D0984064

Growing Up African American in Catholic Schools

Growing Up African American in Catholic Schools

EDITED BY
Jacqueline Jordan Irvine and Michèle Foster

FOREWORD BY JANICE E. JACKSON

Teachers College, Columbia University
New York and London

Published by Teachers College Press, 1234 Amsterdam Avenue, New York, NY 10027

Chapter 4, "Holy Angels: Pocket of Excellence," by Portia H. Shields, originally appeared in the *Journal of Negro Education*, Vol. 58, No. 2 (1989). Reprinted with permission.

Portions of Chapter 10, "I'm Going Home: A Journey to Holy Angels," by William Tate, first appeared in "From Inner City to Ivory Tower: Does My Voice Matter in the Academy?," *Urban Education*, Vol. 29, No. 3 (October 1994). Copyright © 1994 Corwin Press, Inc. Reprinted with permission of Corwin Press.

Library of Congress Cataloging-in-Publication Data

Growing up African American in Catholic schools / edited by Jacqueline Jordan Irvine and Michèle Foster : foreword by Janice E. Jackson.
p. cm.
Includes bibliographical references and index.
ISBN 0-8077-3530-2 (alk. paper)
1. Afro-Americans—Education—United States. 2. Catholic Church—Education—United States. I. Irvine, Jacqueline Jordan. II. Foster, Michèle.
LC2731.G76 1996
377'82—dc20 96-3854
CIP

ISBN 0-8077-3530-2 (cloth)

Printed on acid-free paper
Manufactured in the United States of America

03 02 01 00 99 98 97 96 8 7 6 5 4 3 2 1

There would be no particular need for Catholic schools if the task of education were simply to train and nurture the mind. The fact . . . that Catholic schools promote academic outcomes as well or better than their public counterparts is not sufficient to justify their existence. If Catholic schools are nothing more than cost-efficient promoters of academic achievement, then the Catholic community would be well-advised to reassign the schools' financial and human resources to other areas of need. . . . It is a commitment to heart and spirit, that gives Catholic schools a unique and vital mission. The effective Catholic school is one that nurtures a life-orienting faith; it fulfills an academic purpose and simultaneously produces disposition to service, sparks a passion for justice, and creates commitment to community.

—Benson and Guerra, *Sharing the Faith*

Contents

Foreword

Settling into her desk in the last seat of the first row, she gazed out the window into the blazing sun. Her thoughts were consumed by the discontinuity between a life rich with the customs and traditions of the African American community juxtaposed to a school curriculum that spoke little of this community beyond conversations about "pagan babies" in need of the children's prayers and monetary donations. Though she was only in second grade, she found this place called "school" confusing. She wondered if the goings-on in this institution would ever have any relevance to her real life.

I am that girl in the second grade. I now acknowledge that, indeed, important lessons were learned, which shaped my future success. This volume called me to ponder my own experience as an African American whose success is grounded in the academic achievement and moral foundation of Catholic schooling that supported the values instilled in me at home and in the community. The contributors to this edited work use their own stories to initiate a conversation about the success of one institution in educating many African Americans who went on to make important contributions to the community. The eleven authors present their own experience in Catholic schools as a starting point to help the reader understand the historical and sociological treatment of the education of African Americans in Catholic schools.

This volume comes at a time when many dioceses are choosing to close Catholic schools that serve significant numbers of African American children. May those in positions to make decisions about support for Catholic schools hear the lessons in these pages. Further, the authors challenge the notion that African Americans are unable to rise above the adversity that often accompanies the lives of a people held hostage by racist attitudes and actions. The authors dispel the notion of a people victimized by circumstances that appear to be beyond the community's control. They provide proof of the resilience of a people with a proud history and a hope-filled future. The stories presented here are only a few examples of the many successful individuals who were touched by the commitment of the Catholic Church to educating African Americans.

The stories presented here are interesting in that they are drawn from individuals from a variety of backgrounds. Some were from long-standing Catholic families. Others were converts. Still others were non-Catholic. Some stories speak of life in southern Catholic parishes, while others allow us to peek into northern life. Big cities and small towns provide the backdrop for the stories. The experiences range from schooling in the 1950s to schooling in the late 1980s. Some of the authors were taught by African Americans, while others were taught by whites. Some of the authors attended Catholic schools from the elementary grades through high school. One continued his education into the college seminary. One attended public high school. I enjoyed the rich mixture of their backgrounds. I found it interesting that some common themes ran through the various chapters. The themes are not new. Most of them are ideas that seem to resurface over time. Perhaps this time we will give them the attention that is due. This volume pushes the reader to think beyond the obvious. The lessons learned can be applied to the education of African American students in public schools, not just parochial schools.

The first theme is around high expectations for all students. The role of high expectations by teachers for excellence in student achievement is well documented in other places. The authors make it clear that high expectations for students must be held by all adults in children's lives and must be accompanied by a commonly held responsibility to ensure that all children *will* learn. This responsibility is held by members of the school staff, parents, and the religious communities serving the school and parish. All of the authors gave evidence of the strong commitment to education by African American parents. This commitment is borne out by the sacrifices many of the parents made in order to provide a Catholic school education for their children. Witnessing the commitment of the adults in their lives leads most of the students to accept their own share of the responsibility to do well in school. The second theme focuses on the need for a rigorous curriculum that demonstrates the expectation that the students can learn complex content and master higher-order thinking skills that enable them to make a contribution to the community. The students knew that their success in school was a prerequisite for their success in later life. They were well aware that they lived in a society that, though changing, still did not welcome their success. They were given the clear message that success was nonnegotiable. The third theme was that the support of a nurturing community was essential. For some of the authors, that community was found in a "seamlessness" (Delpit) between home and school, while others remember the pain of a terrible mismatch between their lives at home and school. In these cases, the community that fed their spirits was the African American community outside of the school and church structure of the Roman Catholic Church. The fourth theme centers around the development of a strong identity as an African American. The book gives examples of school communities that managed to incorporate into school life and curriculum the giftedness of African peoples. Yet in other cases the school community attempted to be color blind, thereby denying the value of the students' African ancestry. Some authors speak of families who were clear that the family is ultimately responsible for ensuring that the child develops a strong sense of self as an African American in a society that is often hostile. The family, the African American community, and the Black church were the only sources of racial identity development in these cases. Either choice can stand alone. Neither choice is presented as superior to the other. A fifth theme is the development of the spirit as well as the mind. Many of the authors spoke of character development alongside the rigorous curriculum. Attention to both aspects of human life was important. It is evident that Catholic schools desired well-rounded graduates who carried with them a sense of pride and a commitment to service.

I enjoyed the text because it documents and collects in one place fleeting ideas that are often whispered in the Black community, rarely given credence through formal research. In this volume, the reader is treated to historical analyses of the Catholic Church and its relationship with the African American community. The reader can trace the chronology of the inception and growth of several religious orders founded by African Americans to serve their own community. The reader is treated to an explication of the histories of the various religious orders who chose service to the African American community as their mission work. But an understanding of history is not enough to help the reader learn from the experience of African Americans who were successful in Catholic schools. It was helpful to read an overview of the research studies on the topic.

One can learn a great deal from the individual experiences of the authors. These are the critical pieces of information—the telling of one's own story. The introspection required to reach back provides an opportunity for those who are not educators to grapple with the positive and negative aspects of their own education as they create nurturing experiences for their own students. The various approaches to laying out the lessons provide a full picture. It was a real treat for me to be reminded of the many schools and parishes that took great risks by educating African American children at all. The experiences were not identical, yet they all led to success. As I read this work, I wanted to know more about the depth of the struggles of those students whose success is chronicled here.

Many of the authors scratched the surface; few engaged in a thick description of the struggle. Perhaps that is all that the reader can ask at this time.

The stories that unfold in this volume are an affirmation of the proud work of those who served as teachers and administrators in Catholic schools. They also point to the sacrifices endured by many parents. It was the commitment and perseverance of adults that enabled their children to rise and achieve. This is their success story as well.

I yearned to hear the voices and stories of those whose commitment to African American students made success possible. Absent that, the reader will still close the last page of this volume having been fed by stories of courage. The themes and lessons woven throughout the text are a reminder to the reader that success is the right and responsibility of African Americans. Education is an important vehicle of this achievement.

I am the product of Catholic schools, first grade through my first graduate degree. I felt my own story reflected in this work. Reading this volume brought back memories of an education shaped by rigor and high expectations. It also brought back the feelings of pain and isolation. Overall, my experience in Catholic schools was quite positive. I see the connection between my endeavors there and my endeavors today. Like the authors, I learned a great deal in these institutions. My mind was stretched. Yet my spirit longed for the African American traditions that were withheld from the Catholic community. I participated in Xavier University's program in Black liberation theology in my late 20s and early 30s. It was here that African American educators attended to my mind and spirit in a way that recognized my heritage. That attention compelled me to work for social justice.

Irvine and Foster have placed Catholic schools in the center of the discussion about improving the academic achievement of African American students. The door to this dialogue was barely open. This work blows the door off its hinges and invites educators in both public and parochial schools to participate in a far deeper dialogue.

—Janice E. Jackson

Acknowledgments

An edited volume requires the time, cooperation, and talent of many individuals. We are grateful to the chapter authors for sharing their stories and research and working so diligently in meeting our deadlines. This book would not have been possible without the hard work and assistance of our graduate students Gretchen Peters and Patricia Bell of Emory University and Tryphenia Peele of Claremont Graduate School.

Growing Up African American in Catholic Schools

Introduction

Michèle Foster

The history of this volume began when Jacqueline Jordan Irvine and I met at a conference and, through our conversation, discovered that, although neither of us was Catholic, we had both attended Catholic schools, she in the South and I in the North in the late 1950s through the mid-1960s. Our conversation about our schooling reminded me of the many other African American academics I knew who had also attended Catholic schools. We proposed a symposium for the American Educational Research Association that was so well received that we decided to co-edit this volume. Thus was this book born.

This book is not intended as a romanticized piece about a bygone era, or as an endorsement of Catholic school pedagogy, or as a blueprint for individuals seeking to ameliorate the dismal failure of African American students. We are aware that even the modest cost of Catholic schools places them beyond the reach of many African American families. We are also aware that, like other institutions that are abandoning urban areas, many Catholic schools are also closing their doors. Despite these facts, we know that with limited funds, many Catholic schools continue to offer quality education to substantial and disproportionate numbers of African American students, as reflected in the following data.

Although the Catholic schools of the 1950s were virtually all white, composed of Catholic students from particular ethnic groups, in the 1970s students of color represented 8.2% of Catholic school students. By 1983 this figure had risen to 17.3%, and by 1990 the figure was 22.2%. When compared to the percentage of white and to the percentage of Hispanic students (whose enrollment is larger in Catholic schools than in the public schools), the enrollment of African Americans in Catholic schools is smaller; however, when religious preference is considered, the rate of African American students enrolled in Catholic schools exceeds that of whites or Latinos/Latinas (Bryk, Lee, & Holland, 1993).

Rather than serving as a blueprint for school reform, this volume is intended as a historical and sociological treatment of the education of African Americans in Catholic schools, a topic that is underresearched and poorly understood. The significance of this book is that it challenges dominant educational theory that African Americans, as involuntary minorities and in historical relationship to the dominant community, always respond in predictable ways to the perception of limited opportunities. In addition, it challenges the dominant theory that portrays African Americans as helpless victims in a marginalized culture that exists in constant opposition to Eurocentric beliefs and practices. Despite the racism inherent in the overarching and dominant Eurocentric practices that deny cultural heritage, silence voices, and are often culturally incompatible, African Americans have carved out cultural and political spaces, have shown remarkable resilience, have accommodated without assimilating, and have been able to affirm their identity.

This volume is divided into two sections. The first section contains historical, political, and sociological analyses of the experiences of African Americans in Catholic schools, case studies of Catholic schools, and a literature review of the school achievement of African Americans in Catholic schools. The second section is a set of personal memoirs and reflections written by individuals who attended Catholic schools between the late 1950s and the late 1980s.

In Chapter 1, Darlene Eleanor York reviews the major studies on Catholic schools and the achievement of African American pupils in them. She provides an overview of the enrollment trends of various white ethnic groups and of African American students in Catholic schools over several historical periods, which is particularly useful for understanding contemporary Catholic education in the United States. Her discussion of the three categories of Catholic schools serves as a framework for categorizing the schools described in the personal memoirs that follow. The three categories she discusses are: (1) the parish school financed by a particular parish to educate children from a particular church; (2) the diocesan school financed by a diocese to serve children from several parishes; and (3) the private Catholic school funded by tuition, any tier of the Church hierarchy, or by a religious order of priests, brothers, or nuns. This review also considers the intersection of the background characteristics of students—their families, communities, socioeconomic status, and religious affiliation, as well as the institutional characteristics, curriculum offerings, school size, and per pupil expenditures—of Catholic schools. Tables 1.1–1.5, which summarize 17 major studies conducted between

1973 and 1993 on African American student achievement in Catholic schools, are useful for policy makers and other researchers.

V. P. Franklin, in Chapter 2, provides a self-deterministic, historical overview of the often overlooked role that African Americans have played in organizing Catholic schools and other Catholic institutions on their own behalf. He details the role of individual African American women, such as Maria Becraft, and religious orders of African American women, such as the Oblate Sisters of Providence, in developing schools for Black students. When the Oblate Sisters of Providence, the first Black order of religious women, founded in 1828, opened St. Frances Academy for Colored Girls, attended by Haitian and American Blacks, it was the first school in the city of Baltimore to provide any schooling opportunities for Blacks. Subsequently, the Oblates opened three more schools in Baltimore and two in other cities. Moreover, although he does not provide a detailed history of their order's founding and their efforts in developing Catholic schools for African American students, Franklin mentions the Sisters of the Holy Family in New Orleans and the Franciscan Handmaidens of Mary in Savannah, Georgia.

He also traces the role played by the Committee for the Advancement of Colored Catholics in securing Catholic clergy to minister to the spiritual needs of African American Catholics, providing educational institutions, including institutions of higher education, and exposing and fighting discrimination within the Catholic Church. Although the Committee for the Advancement of Colored Catholics was primarily self-determinist—an organization that would promote unity and cooperation among Black Catholics—the white clergy involved in the organization wanted to redirect the organization's actions toward "interracial activities." This struggle over making Catholic institutions relevant to African Americans continues to this day.

Vernon C. Polite offers a more comprehensive analysis of the Oblate Sisters in Chapter 3. Beginning with their founding of St. Frances Academy in 1828 and continuing up to the present, Polite describes the transition undergone by St. Frances as it developed from an academy for privileged Black girls of Haitian and American descent in the early nineteenth century to a contemporary Catholic coeducational school (as of 1974) designed to serve the need of urban poor African American students. In 1990–91 that school served a student body 30% of whom came from households below the poverty level and 62% of whom lived in single-parent families, statistics that refute the widely held notion that African American students who attend Catholic school come from the most privileged families in the African American community. Despite these background characteristics, which are often linked to school failure and the fact that many of students come with inadequate educational preparations, the majority of students at St. Frances not only go on to postsecondary education but also graduate from them. His description of the school's program reveals that students excel not only academically but also in athletics, as well as being required to do community service by participating in a schoolwide community service project.

In Chapter 4, Portia H. Shields offers a portrait of Holy Angels School on Chicago's Southside. Initially founded by Irish immigrants and attended by their children until the end of World War II, and now headed by Father Paul Smith, Holy Angels School currently serves a student body of 1,300 in grades kindergarten through high school, two-thirds of whom come from the surrounding Southside neighborhood. Shields's chapter focuses on the interlocking and complementary roles played by parents and teachers as they work to insure the success of Holy Angels students, 80% of whom go on to postsecondary education and whose achievement is above national norms in all academic areas. Like students who attend St. Frances Academy in Baltimore, Holy Angels students not only receive a solid academic preparation but also participate in school athletics and engage in community service projects.

The personal reflections of Jacqueline Jordan Irvine (Chapter 5), Michèle Foster (Chapter 6), and Mary E. Dilworth (Chapter 7), all of which occur during the 1950s and 1960s, comprise the first three chapters of the second part and offer interesting comparisons and contrasts. One contrast pertains to the type of Catholic school each attended. Irvine attended Mother Mary Mission in Phenix City, Alabama. Dilworth attended two different ethnically segregated parish schools in the Northeast—St. Mary's, which was predominantly Irish, and St. Bernard's, which was predominantly Italian. Foster first attended a French Catholic parochial school and later a French academy for girls. According to York (Chapter 1), the kind of Catholic institution that Irvine attended was established throughout the South and modeled on the mission schools in Africa. Catholic parish schools developed in response to the increasing immigration of European Catholics that swelled in the 1800s, although student enrollment in these schools fluctuated according to particular ethnic groups and decade. The first academy for girls was founded in New Orleans by the Ursuline Sisters, an order of continental French nuns. A second academy for girls, Visitation, was founded near Georgetown. The creation of academies for girls expanded greatly after 1800, such that by 1830 they were a firmly established type of Catholic institution. They were considered progressive models of education for women when they were founded, and their curriculum consisted of domestic and classical subjects (Bryk, Lee, & Holland, 1993, p. 21). St. Frances Academy, established in 1828 by the Oblate Sisters of Providence, during the height of the period when female religious orders were founding academies, had a curriculum that typified that of other girls' academies (Polite, Chapter 3).

A second contrast in these memoirs is their location; whereas Dilworth and Foster attended predominantly white Catholic schools in the North, Irvine attended an all-Black segregated school in the South.

A third contrast concerns the religious affiliation of the memoirs' authors. Whereas Foster and Irvine were non-Catholics who attended Catholic schools for both their elementary and secondary education, Dilworth was a practicing Catholic who attended Catholic elementary school and later transferred to a public school that was one-third African American. As non-Catholics, Foster and Irvine describe the ways in which their parents embraced certain elements of Catholic schooling while at the same time rejecting those aspects of that same schooling that contradicted their beliefs. But even though her family was Catholic, Dilworth informs us that her parents reinterpreted particular aspects of Catholic teaching that contradicted their own views about salvation. Moreover, despite the pressure that the nuns placed on their elementary students to attend Catholic secondary schools, Dilworth's parents insisted that she attend a public high school where she could interact with African American students, which they felt was a necessary component of her overall education. Taken together these three memoirs represent examples of the development of biculturalism, a search for racial and cultural identity and accommodation without assimilation.

The experiences of Lisa D. Delpit (Chapter 8) and Antoine M. Garibaldi (Chapter 9) took place in Louisiana—in Baton Rouge and New Orleans—where both of them attended elementary schools taught by the Sisters of the Holy Family, the second order of African American religious women founded in the United States (Terborg-Penn, 1993); later Garibaldi attended an African American school run by the Josephite Fathers, a white order of priests who have a long history of working with African American Catholics. Together they present an interesting contrast to the experiences of Irvine, Foster, and Dilworth. Although Garibaldi's experiences took place between 1956 and 1964, and Delpit's between 1959 and 1969, there was a five-year overlap in their attendance dates. Their experiences parallel those of Irvine, Foster, and Dilworth in that the curriculum was entirely Eurocentric. However, Delpit and Garibaldi were Catholic, and they were taught by nuns who shared the same racial and religious background as they. Although this seems to have reduced the religious incongruity, the memoir of Delpit is suffused with the caste system of color and hair texture that valued lighter-skinned students over darker ones, and equated any negative behavior, physicality, or sensuality with the depraved, libidinous, and purient character of African Americans. These negative aspects notwithstanding, percolating through Delpit's and Garibaldi's personal reflections are examples of strong parental support, teachers' belief in their students' abilities, few excuses for unsatisfactory performance, and a clear and explicit purpose for education.

Irrespective of religion, region, or racial background of the religious order that staffed the schools, these five memoirs took place before the civil rights period, a period when African Americans had few expectations of seeing ourselves represented in the school curriculum. One consequence of the civil rights movement was our rising expectation for seeing ourselves depicted and our experiences portrayed in school curricula. These rising expectations can be seen in the memoirs of William Tate (Chapter 10) and Kimberly Ellis (Chapter 11), both of whom attended Catholic schools after the height of civil rights movement. Tate, who began Holy Angels School on the Southside of Chicago as a second grader in 1968 and whose memoir focuses primarily on the positive influence that Father Clements had on the school, uses Black liberation theology to analyze his experiences retrospectively. Through this lens, he interprets Holy Angels as a place where students were empowered "with a knowledge of self and a combative spirit of social reform." The anecdotes he recounts about his experiences at Holy Angels emphasize how the school managed to convey to its students the importance of striving for academic excellence and at the same time the necessity of using this knowledge in the service of self-determination and social justice. Tate's analysis of his own experiences at Holy Angels School is particularly fascinating when compared to the analysis of the same institution rendered in Chapter 4 by Shields, who, despite being African American, is an outsider. These differing perceptions of insider and outsider about which components combined to make Holy Angels an effective school for urban African American students seem to substantiate Tate's claim that individuals hoping to understand the school experiences of African American students must "expand the boundaries of more traditional educational research to include the voices, experiences, and realities of our lives so that a more comprehensive picture of past educational practice can be provided."

Ellis's memoir illustrates how the absence of positive images of African Americans, the omission of the history of African Americans, and, perhaps more important, a lack of "cultural synchronization" (Irvine, 1990) between teachers and pupils can wound even academically able students. Ellis's account of her schooling is disturbing. She believes that her personal identity, racial identity, and cultural background were misunderstood and not appreciated. Despite memories of individual acts of kindness by teachers, a string of academic and extracurricular successes in high school, graduation from a fine undergraduate institution, and matriculation in a master's degree program in English, her account is disturbing.

It is our hope that this volume will move the discussion beyond the current school failure of African Americans to more complex and particularistic insights into how African Americans respond and manipulate political, environmental, and economic situations in order to achieve an education. Finally, it is hoped that these insights will provide readers with new strategies related to how school failure might be reduced and how school success might be achieved for more African American students.

REFERENCES

Bryk, A. S., Lee, V. E., & Holland, P. B. (1993). *Catholic schools and the common good.* Cambridge, MA: Harvard University Press.

Irvine, J. J. (1990). *Black students and school failure: Policies, practices, and prescriptions.* Westport, CT: Greenwood.

Terborg-Penn, R. (1993). Sisters of the Holy Family. In D. C. Hine, E. Barkley-Brown, & R. Terborg-Penn (Eds.), *Black women in America: An historical encyclopedia* (pp. 1040–1041). Bloomington: Indiana University Press.

PART I

Historical and Sociological Analyses of African American Catholic Education

CHAPTER 1

The Academic Achievement of African Americans in Catholic Schools: A Review of the Literature

Darlene Eleanor York

Questions about the academic achievement of African American students have occupied a significant place in educational research literature. Although no easy summary of this research is possible, the experiences of African Americans in U.S. schools seem to lead inescapably to the conclusion that the academic talents of African American students are largely untapped, underutilized, and unrecognized in most academic environments. Many African American students are believed to perform poorly in schools not because they lack sufficient educational opportunities, but because they do not possess sufficient intellectual ability, motivation, or social support. These disadvantages are frequently juxtaposed against a larger, more advantaged Caucasian population. Comparisons of African American students to Caucasian students are informative; they provide clues as to the magnitude of the discrepancies between different populations. However, between-group comparisons have their limitations. A chief drawback is that such comparisons seldom address discrepancies among members of the same population. Thus, although the research on the academic achievement of African Americans is abundant, much of it portrays African American students in comparison to other racial groups rather than exploring differences among groups of African Americans. Within-group comparisons of African Americans in schools have only recently been utilized in educational research designs. This chapter is devoted to an examination of one kind of within-group comparison: dif-

 ISBN 0-8077-3530-2 (cloth).

ferences in academic achievement among African Americans attending public schools versus those attending Roman Catholic schools.

AVAILABILITY OF RESEARCH ON CATHOLIC SCHOOLS AND ACHIEVEMENT

In the 1960s, the Carnegie Corporation provided the major funding for a National Opinion Research Center (NORC) study of Catholic higher education (Greeley & Rossi, 1966). Results from this study were highly favorable to Catholic colleges and universities and sparked an interest in conducting further research on the effects of Catholic schooling. In the early 1980s, two large-scale studies were conducted by the National Center for Education Statistics (NCES) of the U.S. Department of Education. The first, known as the High School and Beyond, or HSB, study, was of a nationally representative sample of high school sophomores and seniors in both public and private schools. This study, headed by Coleman, Hoffer, and Kilgore, provided the data for a series of publications. The best known of these, *Public and Private High Schools* (Coleman, Hoffer, & Kilgore, 1981), generated a great deal of controversy. The criticism was largely directed at two aspects of the study: first, the statistical validity and appropriateness of the analyses; and second, the interpretations of the findings. Several subsequent articles appeared disputing the accuracy and representativeness of the HSB study and urging caution in accepting Coleman, Hoffer, and Kilgore's interpretations of their findings. Such articles appeared in the *Harvard Educational Review* in 1981, in *Educational Researcher* in 1981, in *Phi Delta Kappan* in 1981, and in *Sociology of Education* in 1982, 1983, and 1985. Although the NORC and HSB studies were not directly related, the inclusion of a Catholic school population in both generated additional research interest in Catholic schooling.

In 1982, Father Andrew Greeley, a Roman Catholic priest and sociologist at the University of Chicago, used the HSB data set to test whether one population of students—minority students—in one type of private school—Catholic schools—showed any significant differences in academic achievement from minority students in public schools (Greeley, 1982). Again, however, the use of the HSB data set drew fire from critics, who charged that the sample of Catholic and other private schools used in the HSB study was insufficient, self-selected, and did not represent private education in the United States. More importantly, the critics argued that any conclusions about differences in the selectivity of school populations (e.g., whether populations in private schools self-select as an elitist group and thus perpetuate social distances along class, gender, and racial lines) or academic achievement were largely unwarranted (Bryk, Lee, & Holland, 1993). Despite the criticisms, Greeley's arguments about the effects of Catholic schooling on minority students demanded further research. Greeley found that minority students in Catholic schools achieved far greater academic gains than minority students in public schools. Furthermore, the gains were inversely proportional to the minority student's level of "advantage." Minority students who were from the lowest income levels, had the poorest academic records, and were at the greatest level of risk had the highest relative rates of achievement (Greeley, 1982).

Toward the end of 1982, a second HSB data set was collected using the same population of students that had been studied in 1980. This second study provided a longitudinal view of these students: the 1980 sophomores were now seniors; the seniors were now two years past graduation. Although criticism about the characteristics of the sample, the analyses, and the interpretations of the findings persisted, the second HSB study did answer important questions about the effects of schooling over time. For example, one controversy surrounding the findings of the first HSB study centered on whether the effects of private schooling might be attributable to differences in the background of the students rather than to the advantages of a private education. Specifically, although the first HSB data set might show that sophomores in private schools had higher academic achievement scores than sophomores in public schools, there was no measure of the rate of achievement. Perhaps students currently enrolled in private schools entered those private schools with advanced achievement levels, thus eliminating the effects of private schooling. The second HSB data set, by measuring the same students over time, could more accurately measure the effects of schooling (Coleman & Hoffer, 1987).

On the whole, much of the research generated within the last 15 years has been in response to these landmark studies. Thus any review of the recent research on the academic achievement of any students in Catholic schools, including African American students, must necessarily address both the problematic and the promising features of these and other subsequent large-scale studies. Little research utilizing smaller, more discrete populations of students in Catholic schools has been conducted. Hence a literature review reflects both the contributions and limitations of topics researchers have chosen to pursue, the status of the research on Catholic schools given the ambiguous results of some of the studies, and the dominance of theoretical approaches used to assess African American achievement. Research on achievement in Catholic schools has been guided more by the perception of differences in climate, curricula, and community between Catholic and non-Catholic schools than by general theoretical principles, differences in instruction, or comparisons of teacher characteristics (Bryk, Holland, Lee, & Carriedo, 1984; Bryk, Lee, & Holland, 1993).

Recognizing these constraints, this review addresses what is known about African American achievement in Catholic schools in order to specify the parameters of existing research and to define directions for new research. The review is organized around three distinct topics: (1) a brief summary of the history of Catholic schooling for minority students, the assumptions that direct this research, and the relevance of these assumptions to achievement constructs; (2) the measurement of achievement among African American Catholic school students and the implicit assumptions that guide the definition, operationalization, and interpretations of achievement; and (3) an examination of the ways in which findings on African American achievement have appealed or have failed to appeal to the research and practitioner communities.

Both manual and computerized searches of educational, psychological, and sociological abstracts through 1993 were conducted to establish a literature basis for the review. These searches uncovered three broad kinds of research: studies of the history of Catholic education in the United States, studies surrounding nationally representative measures conducted by public and Catholic school researchers, and other studies of achievement united by the inclusion of Catholic school students in the sample population. The difficulty of organizing this research lay not in separating unrelated research but in broadening the categories for examining existing research. The inconsistency of theoretical approaches, the controversy surrounding existing quantitative analyses, and the insufficiency of information regarding effect sizes in many of the older studies dictated the use of a traditional qualitative review rather than a more technical quantitative method, such as meta-analysis. The review concludes with a discussion of our knowledge of experiences of African American students in Catholic schools, the limitations of our knowledge, and suggestions for future research.

CATHOLIC SCHOOLS AND THE EDUCATION OF MINORITY STUDENTS

Compared to the knowledge we have about the history of public schools in the United States, relatively little is known about the history of Catholic school education. The proliferation of parish schools in major cities such as Boston, New York, and Chicago is well-documented (Dolan, 1981;

Sanders, 1977), as are many of the battles waged between Catholics and non-Catholics over the issues of tax-supported schooling (Hunt & Kunkel, 1988; Lazerson, 1977). However, relatively little is known about the kinds of teaching and learning that occurred inside Catholic schools or the response of the parents and community to the education their children received. This lack of knowledge doubtless stems from a longstanding lack of interest by the non-Catholic educational research community and from the scarcity of Catholic researchers whose interests lay in educational history (Greeley & Rossi, 1966).

Shortly after the end of World War II, a number of Catholic intellectuals formed the Catholic Commission on Intellectual and Cultural Affairs, an organization headed by the Reverend William Rooney of the Catholic University of America. The purpose of the commission was to evaluate and describe the intellectual and educational life of Catholics in America. Two volumes were published under the auspices of the organization—Ellis's *American Catholics and the Intellectual Life* (1956) and O'Dea's *The American Catholic Dilemma* (1958). Both of these works were highly critical of education in parochial schools and portrayed American Catholics as decidedly anti-intellectual. Although Ellis had used pre–World War II data to substantiate his arguments, and O'Dea had written a theoretical rather than empirical piece, the findings from these studies were unchallenged. In fact, the conclusions drawn from these studies seemed to align so well with the general sentiment of the time that the intellectual inferiority of Catholic elementary and secondary schools became axiomatic (Greeley, 1982). However, the findings of the 1960s NORC study, a study of Catholic higher education (Greeley & Rossi, 1966), and, more recently, the results of several large-scale studies have challenged this common lore of Catholic educational inferiority so thoroughly that a new interest in the processes and outcomes of Catholic education has arisen among educational researchers.

One aspect of this interest has been the education of minority students in Catholic schools. While recent studies do suggest that the academic achievement of minority students in Catholic schools significantly surpasses that of minority students in public schools, these findings are often cited without reference to the historical context in which this education occurred. Thus assumptions about the climate of Catholic schools, parental involvement, social class, and teaching styles are not informed by a knowledge of how Catholic schools educated minorities throughout U.S. history. This historical perspective, however, provides an important context for our current understanding of the achievement of African American students in Catholic schools and for our assessment of the research on minority achievement that has been conducted to date.

The Cultural Context of Catholic Education

Catholic schools consist primarily of three subtypes: (1) the parish school—financed by the members of a single church, the school educates children of families who attend that church; (2) the diocesan school—financed by the diocese, the school educates children from several area parishes; (3) the private Catholic school—financed by any hierarchical tier of the Catholic Church, by tuition, or by a religious order of nuns, priests, or brothers, the private Catholic school differs from the parish and diocesan schools. Frequently, for example, the admission criteria, curricula, and traditions are not formed in reference to the other Catholic schools in the area (Bryk et al., 1993). The private Catholic school is more independent in its financial base and in its function than the other types of Catholic schools.

The popularity and strength of these types of Catholic schools in the Unites States prior to World War II traditionally followed the ebb and flow of immigration. For example, between 1830 and 1880, the size of the Catholic population grew from 500,000 to more than 8 million, and the number of parish schools grew rapidly. The number of parish schools, however, did not grow concurrently. For example, despite the fact that more than half of the city of Boston was Catholic by 1880, fewer than 10 percent of the city's children were enrolled in Catholic schools (Perko, 1987).

Furthermore, there were differences in minority and ethnic group responses to Catholic education. These groups varied in their religious commitment to and financial support of Catholic schools. German Catholic immigrants, for example, founded Catholic schools in almost every parish, often building schools before churches. Irish Catholics were less assiduous in establishing parish schools, and Italian Catholics still less so. An explanation of this phenomenon that relies on differences in language (e.g., the Irish were less eager to found schools because they spoke the language of the public school) is undermined by the presence of Italian-speaking immigrants who did not establish their own parish schools. For example, "by the end of the century, Poles outnumbered [Italians] by two to one, but had thirteen times as many schools" (Sanders, 1977). Thus the social ecology that contributed to Catholic parish school formation was undoubtedly the result of a variety of cultural, as well as religious, influences.

In the years prior to World War I, the popularity of Catholic schools waned and did not flourish again until the advent of World War II and the subsequent baby boom. By 1966, the number of students in elementary and secondary Catholic schools reached a high of 5.6 million and constituted 87% of non–public school enrollment (Hunt & Kunkel, 1988). After 1966, however, the numbers of students and the percentage of non–public school enrollment declined. By 1982, Catholic school students accounted for only 64 percent of non–public school enrollment (Hunt & Kunkel, 1988). Despite fluctuations in enrollment, by the middle of the twentieth century Catholic school enrollment could no longer be explained by differences among immigrant groups. Catholic school students uniformly spoke English and attended schools that, from an institutional perspective, resembled public schools in administrative design, teacher characteristics, and school policy.

Nor could the differences be explained by changes in popes or papal policy. The United States was the only modernized country in the world that maintained a nationwide denominational school system without governmental funding (Greeley & Rossi, 1966). Thus, when the pope or his representatives spoke of the education of Catholic youth, the directives were filtered through a vast, decentralized, uneven system of U.S. bishops, priests, nuns, and parents. This multiplicity of perspectives—despite the central unifying factor of Catholic Church membership—resulted in somewhat liberal interpretations of Church directives about schooling. At times, Church directives were ignored or resisted. For example, in 1880, 94% of the parishes in Baltimore had parish schools. Church leaders met that year and ordered that every church should build a school. However, within six years of the order, the number had dramatically dropped: only 77 percent of the parishes had schools (Sanders, 1977). In 1929 Pope Pius XI issued the Christian Education of Youth encyclical making the Catholic education of Catholic children compulsory. Ironically, within a decade, Catholic school enrollment dropped for the first time in U.S. history (Dolan, 1985). Nevertheless, in some parishes, the pressure to enroll children in parish schools was so great that priests refused absolution, Eucharist, and other sacraments to parents who did not enroll their children (Hunt & Kunkel, 1988).

African Americans in Catholic Schools

When public schools began to integrate after the *Brown v. Board of Education* decision of 1954, once-stable urban and near-urban residential areas experienced "white flight." Of course, parochial schools were not legally affected by the Supreme Court's decision and were free to remain segregated. However, Catholic parents, following the changing residential trends of public school parents, began to move to the suburbs, thus abandoning urban and inner-city Catholic schools to minority students. Urban Catholic schools began to fill with African American and Hispanic students left behind in the wake of the Caucasian exodus to the suburbs (Perko, 1987). During the first waves of minority student influx into Catholic schools, many urban parishes resisted the minority groups (Bryk et al., 1993). In Chicago, for example, African Americans—both Catholic and non-Catholic—were confined to one parish school where they were allowed to receive the sacraments and attend school. Over time, African American Catholics were allowed to receive the sacraments at any Catholic church, but they were still confined to one parish school. Archbishop George Mundelein of Chicago, a leader in Catholic education, drew a sharp distinction between African American membership in the Church and African American attendance in Catholic schools. He maintained that while the church doors of Chicago were open to African Americans, the school doors were not (Sanders, 1977).

Other parishes saw the influx of African Americans as an opportunity for evangelism and conversion. In many parochial schools, as many as 66% of new Catholic school enrollees identified themselves as non-Catholic; by graduation, the number who self-identified as Catholics had grown to 95% (Sanders, 1977). Although few schools were built specifically for African Americans, Catholic schools integrated neither slowly nor evenly. As in public schools, once Catholic school doors opened to African American students, the schools typically became either wholly African American or they remained almost exclusively Caucasian (Sanders, 1977).

However, urban schools were not the only places where African American students received a Catholic education. After a long and influential program of missionary work and missions schooling in Africa, the Catholic Church turned its attention toward African Americans living in rural areas. Using the model for mission schools that had been successful in many parts of Africa, the Catholic Church established "mission" schools for African Americans throughout the South (Cremin, 1988).

Catholic schools tend to have a large percentage of African American students relative to the entire Catholic student population (Coleman, Hoffer, & Kilgore, 1982). Catholic schools also tend to have a significantly larger proportion of African American students than do other private schools (Kraushaar, 1972). Nonetheless, the percentages of African American students enrolled in Catholic schools is significantly lower than those enrolled in public schools, and the underrepresentation of African Americans has remained consistent since the 1960s (Convey, 1989). Although the numbers of African Americans enrolled in Catholic schools declined more than 20% between 1982 and 1989, this decline is more compelling when viewed against the total numbers of students enrolled in the United States at any given time (Convey, 1989). Condon (1984), for example, found that in 1984 only 7% of the nation's sophomores were enrolled in private schools; of those, only 3% attended Catholic schools. Hence, the numbers of African Americans exposed to a Catholic school education is quite small and is shrinking.

African Americans who attend Catholic schools tend to conform to other demographic profiles. For example, African American students tend to enroll in Catholic schools whether or not they are Catholic and whether or not they are members of any particular social class. Coleman and Hoffer (1987) found that African American students, Catholic and non-Catholic, were as likely to attend Catholic schools as Caucasian students even if African American family incomes were lower. Additionally, African Americans in urban areas and in the Southeast are more likely to attend Catholic schools than African Americans in rural or suburban areas outside the Southeast (Bredeweg, 1985). Benson, Yeager, Guerra, and Manno (1986), in a study of Catholic high schools, found that African American students are more likely to attend smaller rather than larger schools, are more likely to attend single-gender rather than coeducational schools, and are more likely to attend schools in the midwestern, southeastern, and Great Lakes regions of the United States.

The Catholic Response to African American Education

From all appearances, the resistance of the Catholic Church to welcoming African Americans into parish schools, the movement of Catholic parents to suburban areas after the *Brown* decision, and the negligence of the church in creating racially integrated parish schools seems to mimic the Caucasian public school community in its racially separatist attitude and action. However, the Church's seeming resistance to the harmonious integration of Catholic schools should be placed in a larger historical perspective. By the middle 1950s, when the *Brown* decision was made, the Catholic Church in the United States already had a long history of educating numerous cultural and ethnic groups. Throughout that history, never did the Catholic Church engineer the assimilation of any ethnic group in the United States. On the contrary, Catholic educational history—from a cultural perspective—has been tolerant and supportive of separatist schooling.

For example, although the universal Catholic Church was united by a Latin liturgy until Vatican II, the Church had traditionally supported cultural distinctiveness in spiritual expression. Differences in the language of the homily as well as in architectural styles and music reflected national and ethnic preferences. When immigrants arrived in the United States from a variety of predominantly Catholic nations, they were rebuffed by a "public" school system that welcomed neither their language, their culture, their values, nor their religion. Hence, the creation of Catholic schools seemed a cultural, if not an academic, necessity. However, the presence of Catholic schools—often combining different Catholic ethnic groups—created the potential for tremendous tension among religiously uniform but ethnically distinct groups (Hunt & Kunkel, 1988; Lazerson, 1977; Sanders, 1977).

In response, the Catholic Church allowed the creation of "national" parishes and schools. Therefore, in one city or neighborhood there might be dozens of different Catholic churches and schools, each representing a different Catholic ethnic group with its own culture, language, and traditions. This national and ethnic separatism permeated the Church so deeply that nuns and monks sometimes would not share a convent or monastery with religious persons of other cultural groups. Furthermore, this practice dominated all levels of Church life despite any declines in the size or economic resources of a particular group. The distinctions between the groups were so entrenched that even if a parish were shrinking beyond its capacity for meaningful operation, merging with another parish of a different culture was out of the question. "Thus . . . the German school had 1,172 pupils; the Lithuanian, only 175. . . . Yet for a Pole or Lithuanian or Slovak to attend St. Rose before the last Irish child had departed was unthinkable" (Sanders, 1977, p. 244). A tempest occurred at one point when a Lithuanian school, unable to transport nuns from Lithuania quickly enough to meet staffing needs, complained that the Polish nuns who were sent to teach were converting their Lithuanian children into Poles (Sanders, 1977).

Thus the history of Catholic education in the United States can be seen as the history of a well-orchestrated separatist movement. From a public school perspective, it appears that Catholics uniformly rejected what they considered the Protestant and secular slant of public education in favor of the solidarity of a united ecclesiastical and educational system. From the Catholic perspective, however, a very different picture emerges. Regardless of the financial, political, or cultural benefits that might have accrued from a united American Catholic church, parish schools were allowed to flourish and fade within dozens of small ethnic communities. Catholics feared not only the taint of public education, but the taint of Catholic education that did not bear the unique print of their cultural identity.

As long as national parishes existed, the Catholic Church defended their existence and allowed for educational self-determination (Sanders, 1977). This tradition of respecting other cultures and giving them voice, visibility, and power in their schools became the model for the education of African Americans in the 1960s. No attempt was made by Church authorities to keep the Caucasian population in urban areas or to integrate Catholic schools. Instead, the long history of separatist education and cultural distinctiveness dictated that African American Catholic schools, even if they did not arise from African American parishes, would be accorded the same right to separate themselves and to receive an education that dozens of different ethnic and minority groups had received before them. It is in this context of cultural separatism that the academic achievement of African Americans becomes meaningful.

CATHOLIC SCHOOLS AND AFRICAN AMERICAN ACADEMIC ACHIEVEMENT

Research on the academic achievement of students in Catholic schools can be seen in two stages. The first stage occurred roughly between 1965 and 1980. In 1965, when Greeley's (Greeley & Rossi, 1966) NORC findings were published, the Catholic educational research community began to explore schooling outcomes. Funded primarily by the National Catholic Educational Association (NCEA), studies were conducted on a wide range of Catholic educational issues, including the education of African Americans and other minorities in Catholic schools. Little interest in Catholic schooling outside the Catholic research community existed until 1980, when the first HSB study was conducted. In 1980, a second stage of research activity began. This research has focused national attention on the outcomes of Catholic education.

Much of this research suggests not only that Catholic schools are effective but that they are more effective than public schools, particularly more effective for the education of African American students. Although research on these findings continues, researchers have suggested that the positive outcomes for minority students are attributable, in part, to a Catholic school climate characterized by order, discipline, high academic expectations, a caring and committed teaching faculty, and high levels of parental interest and involvement (Bryk et al., 1984; Coleman & Hoffer, 1987). The exploration of variables related to school climate stems largely from a U.S. Department of Education initiative in the 1980s to fund studies on character, choice, and curriculum in schools. These variables have also been explored by a parallel stream of Catholic-based funding, primarily from the NCEA and the Catholic League for Religious and Civil Rights.

Table 1.1 summarizes selected characteristics of the studies used to form this review. Indicated in the table are components of the studies

TABLE 1.1. Major Studies of African American Achievement in Catholic Schools

Year	Author(s)	Funding Source/Sponsor	Sample Characteristics	Variables Examined	Summary of Findings
1973	Madaus & Linnan		Elementary schoolchildren in Catholic and public schools	IQ Attendance	CS>PS
1975	Miller & Kavanagh		All-female Catholic high school 49% AA; 49% CA Students and parents surveyed	Implications of resegregation	50% AA parents felt daughters benefited from attending integrated school; 73% CA parents felt daughters' academic achievement would be strengthened in all-CA school
1979	Vitullo-Martin	U.S. Catholic Conference	Inner-city Catholic schools	Funding, enrollment rates, regional migration, facilities	Inner-city parishes losing money; closing inner-city CS leaves poor and minority children without further options for Catholic education
1981	Coleman, Hoffer, & Kilgore/HSB	NORC/Center for Education Statistics	Stratified, national sample of >30,000 sophomores and >28,000 seniors	Academic performance School-related variables Home variables Aspirations	AACS>AAPS
1982	Cibulka, O'Brien, & Zewe	Catholic League for Religious and Civil Rights	54 Title I schools with a minority enrollment <54% 4,000 parents, 300 teachers, and 50 principals	Parental expectations Faculty and administrative motivation Religious value Family SES Recruiting faculty	AACS>AAPS

1982	Coleman, Hoffer, & Kilgore/HSB	National Center for Education Statistics	Follow-up of 1980 HSB data set	Family SES Race/ethnicity Educational attainments Working patterns of mother Importance of religion to mother/father Parental involvement in school Student participation in extra-curricular activities Expenditures by school per pupil School size School participation in federal programs Curriculum offerings Tracking	CS>PS AACS<CACS AACS>AAPS
1982	Greeley/HSB	NORC/Center for Education Statistics	All 7,000 AA Catholic students enrolled in 1982 and a random sample of 7,000 AA public school students drawn from HSB	Same as HSB 1980	AACS>AAPS AACS<HSCS

(continued)

TABLE 1.1 (continued)

Year	Author(s)	Funding Source/Sponsor	Sample Characteristics	Variables Examined	Summary of Findings
1984	Byrk, Holland, Lee, & Carriedo	Chief administrators of the National Catholic Educational Association	All Catholic high schools used in HSB 1980 study plus extensive field data from 7 Catholic high schools and 13 Catholic elementary schools HSB 1982 plus data from 7 Catholic high schools (considered to be nonelite) and 13 feeder Catholic elementary schools	Curriculum Religious education Teacher expectations School discipline Academic attitudes/ behaviors Reading Mathematics I and II Academic emphasis throughout school Academic expectations Curriculum offerings Discipline policies and frequency of problems Emphasis on religion Sense of community Teacher beliefs Teacher commitment Parental involvement in school	AACS<CACS AACS>AAPS Emphasis on traditional academic curriculum; common value system and developmental religion courses; high academic expectations for all students; teachers personally involved with students and viewed teaching as a ministry; high levels of student engagement and few disruptive incidents; schools selected by higher-income families for academic reasons and by lower-income families for religious reasons
1986	Benson et al.	Ford Foundation and NCEA	Administrators from >1,200 Catholic high schools representing 80% of U.S. Catholic high schools 106 Catholic high schools whose student bodies were more than 50% AA or HS, and which reported that at least 10% of the students lived below the poverty line 7,500 freshmen and seniors enrolled in 106 Catholic high schools where at least 10% of the families met federal poverty guidelines and 900 teachers from these schools	Academic performance Faith development Religious community development Race/ethnicity Family SES Religious affiliation of student School vandalism Sense of community Faith commitment of student Global awareness Discipline policies of school Teacher's membership in religious order Comparison with 1983 study	Emphasis on academic performance and curriculum; higher teacher turnover rates than in public high schools; smaller enrollments per school than in public high schools AACS<HSCS AACS<CACS Low-income schools have higher proportion of religious on staff than middle-income Catholic schools; low-income students had equal access to academic curriculum as middle-income Catholics except in areas of mathematics and science

1987	Coleman & Hoffer/HSB longitudinal data	NORC/Center for Education Statistics	Follow-up from HSB 1980	Same as HSB 1980 and dropout rates and rates of retention in higher education	AACS>AAPS
1987	Lee	NAEP	Nationally representative sample of students in grades 4, 8, and 11	Educational attainments of parent(s) Demographic characteristics Geographic region	Neither CS nor PS students score well in writing; CS students write better than PS students at all three grade levels; AACS and HSCS score below CACS at all three grade levels, and the gap between scores is larger in writing than in reading
1989	Lee & Stewart	NCEA	1,900 3rd-, 7th-, and 11th-grade students; mathematics and science proficiency in CS drawn from larger 1983–84 NAEP data	Race/ethnicity Level of parental education Geographic location of CS Gender	CS>PS at all three grade levels in both mathematics and science
1989	Marks & Lee	NAEP	16,000 students in grades 3, 7, and 11	Family background Individual characteristics School climate and program	At all three grade levels, CS scores are higher than PS; furthermore, gaps widen as age increases
1993	Bryk, Lee, & Holland	NCEA	Randomly selected subset of HSB data from 401 schools plus fieldwork at 7 Catholic high schools considered to be nationally representative	School climate/program and teacher characteristics	Achievement measures for minority students significantly higher in Catholic schools; attributable to sense of community, high level of student engagement, and absence of disruptive behaviors

Note: The following abbreviations are used throughout the table: AA=African American HS=Hispanic CA=Caucasian CS=Catholic school PS=Public school

considered important to the interpretation of results. For example, by including the funding source/sponsor for each study, a delineation of the kind of research conducted by Catholic agencies is distinguishable from research designed outside the Church. It is important to note that, while all of these studies show favorable outcomes for African Americans in Catholic schools, the variables selected for measurement differ widely. This variation and diversity of independent variables suggested a more convenient grouping should be created. For this reason, the variables are grouped into three broad strands: family background/parental characteristics, student/demographic characteristics, and school climate/program and teacher characteristics. These strands are identified and grouped in Table 1.2. Using the groupings created in Table 1.2, a more thorough analysis of each of these dimensions is possible.

Methodological Issues and Concerns

Despite the numbers of large-scale studies that have been conducted through the years, research on Catholic schools and achievement has not been immune from a variety of methodological criticisms. Chief among these criticisms is that the design of the studies has been flawed and the conclusions flowing from the analysis of the data are in error proportionate to the magnitude of the flaws. A brief summary of the kinds of methodological criticisms that have been leveled against research on Catholic school education follows.

Design. One of the central difficulties with Catholic school research, specifically research on African American students within Catholic schools, has been the issue of population comparability. So few African American students attend Catholic schools—and their numbers decrease as they progress through the grade levels—that comparing them to the general population of African American students enrolled in public schools is difficult. Some believe that the inordinate discrepancies of size between African American public and Catholic school populations mitigate against any real generalizability of results (Keith & Page, 1985).

A second design difficulty surrounds the choice of variables used to capture and measure achievement and its correlates. Large-scale studies that employ standardized tests (particularly the National Assessment of Educational Progress [NAEP], HSB, and Iowa Test of Basic Skills [ITBS] measures) are necessarily vulnerable to the charge that some other unmeasured domain of achievement would yield different results. Perhaps African American public students gain some attribute of critical or creative thinking not accessible to Catholic students; perhaps an aspect of

TABLE 1.2. Summary of Major Variables Examined for Impact on African American Achievement in Catholic Schools

Family Background/Parental Characteristics	Student/Demographic Characteristics	School Climate/Program and Teacher Characteristics
Academic expectations of father	Achievement motivation	Academic emphasis throughout school
Academic expectations of mother	Amount of dating	Academic expectations
Educational attainments of parent(s)	Amount of homework done	Administrators' membership in religious order
Family income	Amount of television viewed	Curriculum offerings
Family configuration	Educational aspirations	Curriculum tracking
Family life characteristics	Gender	Discipline policies and frequency of problems
Family size	Geographic region—areas of country /county/city	Emphasis on religion
Frequency of religious activities in the home	Self-perceived educational ability	Morale
Importance of religion to father	Self-perceived value of college education	Placement in academic track
Importance of religion to mother	Participation in extracurricular activities	Placement in vocational track
Parental aspirations for child(ren)	Race/ethnicity	Sense of community
Working patterns of mother	Years consecutively attended Catholic schools	Sense of nurturing
Catholic/non-Catholic affiliation	IQ	Teacher beliefs
	Religious affiliation	Teacher commitment
	Global awareness	Teacher experiences
	Faith commitment	Teachers' membership in religious order
		Teacher training
		Expenditures per pupil
		School size
		Parental involvement in school

intelligence or achievement too subtle for standardized tests generates incomplete results. Furthermore, most of the achievement measures have focused on reading and mathematics. Other areas of achievement, particularly in the sciences—an area Bryk and colleagues (1993) found to be particularly weak in Catholic schools—or in music, that might yield different results have been largely unexplored. Finally, in a few studies, school grades or even parents' perceptions of student achievement have been used as achievement measures, although generalizability from these variables is severely limited.

Aside from the difficulty of determining how to measure achievement, other variables have proven troublesome as well. For example, that parents of Catholic school children *choose* this education for their children is self-evident. Frequently, the act of choosing a private education for their children and the constellation of emotional, social, academic, and vocational expectations assumed to be inherent in the choice for private education are invoked as an explanation for differences in student achievement between public school and Catholic school students. However, this argument necessarily leads to the conclusion that public school parents do not choose an adequate or advanced education for their children, that African American public school parents are passive, negligent, and unconcerned about the education of their children (at least, less concerned than African American parents who choose Catholic education). This conclusion, currently unsubstantiated by the educational experiences of other ethnic groups, is unwarranted. Furthermore, even if choice proves to be an ascendant variable, it cannot be the sole variable. Doubtless other factors enhance the effect. (A more complete treatment of the issue of parental choice in Catholic education can be found in Bryk and colleagues [1993].)

The definition and operationalization of other variables are equally difficult. For example, many of these studies employ social class as a variable. However, there is no standardization of this variable across the studies. In one study, the principal's perception of the relative poverty of students was used as a measure of social class (Benson et al., 1986). Furthermore, the ways in which social-class status, achievement, and other important variables (such as parental aspirations and school climate) are operationalized have made cross-study comparisons difficult.

Analysis and Interpretation. The manipulation of achievement variables using statistical procedures makes the data vulnerable to the weaknesses of quantitative analysis. For example, the reliance on the arithmetic mean forces the loss of other data configurations. In addition, the choice of which variables to measure and how to conduct the statistical analyses determine, to some extent, the outcomes. Finally, the question of which aspects of achievement may be most strongly related to other aspects of school experience limits the studies.

Discovering factors that enhance achievement among African American students in Catholic schools has been challenging. In the last decade, for example, the research on African American achievement has shifted in focus from a predominantly curriculum-based exploration to one centered largely on variables related to school climate. These climate-related factors, however, prove somewhat resistant to quantification. Is there a "typical" Catholic school climate that contributes to academic success more effectively than the "typical" public school climate? If so, then the notion that schools are unique communities of learning that shape distinctive patterns of achievement is suspect. Furthermore, if a typical Catholic school climate creates academic success, then not merely the identification but the extrapolation of these variables into public institutions seems necessary. However, Greeley and Rossi (1966), Coleman and Hoffer (1987), and others have suggested that the crucial climate factor in Catholic education is the presence of an active and well-defined religious value system—clearly a climate-related variable inaccessible to public schools. Hence the interpretation of the results of these comparative studies is difficult.

Sampling Procedures. Many large-scale studies utilizing a Catholic school population have drawn from nationally representative student samples, thus enabling researchers to gain an understanding of educational trends on a broad scale. Over time, these national studies have changed. They have, for example, shifted in focus from student-centered to school-centered areas of exploration. This adjustment in focus helps to refine variables and thus specify effects. However, problems with sampling procedures persist. For example, the preponderance of studies have been conducted on high school populations; few studies have addressed the impact of Catholic education on the achievement of elementary school children.

Summary of Methodological Issues. While the research on Catholic education has drawn criticism regarding a variety of methodological issues, the criticism reflects more the need for additional research rather than the need to dismiss what has already been learned through several decades of research. Obviously, because the population of African American students in Catholic schools is so small, nationally representative samples have aided scholars examining the experiences of these students in ways that single-site, or single-area, studies would not. Nonetheless, the research results—because of various design flaws—are somewhat ambiguous, and additional research designed to overcome these criticisms is needed.

MAJOR STUDIES OF AFRICAN AMERICAN ACHIEVEMENT IN CATHOLIC SCHOOLS

Table 1.1 summarizes the major research studies of Catholic schools in the last two decades that have included African American students in the population sample. Some trends in research designs can be seen. For example, regarding the three groups of variables mentioned in Table 1.2 (family background/parental characteristics, student/demographic characteristics, and school climate/program and teacher characteristics), only a relatively few studies have concentrated on individual and demographic variables. Fewer still have focused on family background variables. Most studies have emphasized school climate and program characteristics. The relative absence of family and individual characteristics may reflect the difficulty of standardizing these variables adequately within national samples. Nonetheless, the relative interest in school-related variables suggests that—despite individual characteristics and the power of the family in shaping achievement—the research community has chosen to explore school-related issues far more thoroughly than any other constellation of variables related to achievement.

Interestingly, while virtually all studies conducted in the 1970s and 1980s included school-related variables in the examination of African American achievement, the 1980s studies examined a narrowed and more precise set of variables. For example, studies in the 1970s might include a list of courses offered by Catholic schools (such as calculus and advanced placement [AP] English) and measure achievement among African American students relative to the number of students who enrolled in and completed this advanced coursework. In the 1980s, studies more frequently included a wider variety of school-related variables—such as an examination of teacher attitudes, an estimate of the percentage of faculty who were members of religious orders, or the measured importance placed on students attending religious retreats—in the search for variables related to achievement.

Although the number of studies conducted on Catholic school academic achievement has been increasing in recent years, the number of these studies that include African American students is quite small. Of these, most are comparative studies—that is, they are studies that compare African American students to Caucasian students enrolled in public or Catholic schools. Only two studies have examined minority students exclusive of any other population. The first was Greeley's study, mentioned earlier (Greeley, 1982). The second was a 1985 follow-up of the 1982 HSB study conducted by Keith and Page (1985), who had used only African American and Hispanic students from the 1982 sample. Only two studies have specifically examined minority populations and social-class levels. The first, a 1983 Ford Foundation and National Catholic Education Association study, examined more than 80% of Catholic high schools nationwide and related family background variables, including family income, to academic achievement. The second, a National Catholic Education Association (1985) study, drew from 106 Catholic high schools where the student population was more than 50% African American or Hispanic and where at least 10% of the students were reported to live below the poverty line (Benson et al., 1986).

In general, the research literature on African Americans in Catholic education seems to reflect a concern with the general effects of private education rather than the specific classroom experiences or teaching strategies that contribute to achievement. The research is undoubtedly thorough and the analyses are credible—despite the methodological criticisms mentioned earlier—and more than two decades of research has been conducted using similar constructs, populations, and analytical tools. The later studies largely confirm earlier findings. The research has been progressively refined through the introduction of new variables. However, the gains in our knowledge seem relatively small; our understanding of the phenomenon of Catholic schooling in the lives of African American children has not increased significantly in recent years.

Family Background/Parental Characteristics

In recent research, the relationship of family background to student academic achievement has been underscored by the work of Coleman (1981) and others who suggest that parental involvement and interest are critical factors in the success of students. The assumption is that parents whose homes and family relationships are stable and who are active participants in the schooling process tend to produce more academically successful children. When children come from impoverished backgrounds or broken homes, the rates of achievement in public schools decline. Children who fit this profile and who are members of a minority group are assumed to face nearly insurmountable obstacles to academic achievement. Children whose family backgrounds and parental characteristics fail to conform to mainstream attributes are at risk in public education. Does the same at-risk profile emerge for these children in Catholic schools? In other words, do poor and minority children face the same obstacles to academic achievement in Catholic schools as poor and minority children in public schools?

Table 1.3 was designed to answer this question by examining the research that has addressed these background issues. The studies in this group primarily measured the impact of family background in the lives of high school students. The age and maturity of this group may mitigate against the measure of family influence in education, since the strongest family effects might occur earlier in a student's life. Only one study has examined only an elementary population (Cibulka, O'Brien, & Zewe, 1982); two other National Assessment of Educational Progress (NAEP) studies (Lee & Stewart, 1989; Marks & Lee, 1989) included third graders in a large pool of seventh and eleventh graders.

The search for family background elements that may contribute to achievement reflects both standard and somewhat unusual approaches. For example, most studies include parental educational levels, parental incomes, parental aspirations, and maternal employment as variables for examination. A few recent studies have included parents' religious affiliation, number of material objects in the home, and parental participation in school events as variables for examination as well.

The findings from these studies show an interesting aspect of Catholic education and its effects on students. For example, in an early study of a Catholic high school experiencing integration, Miller and Kavanagh (1975) found that both Caucasian and African American parents believed their children's social skills were enhanced by attending an integrated school. However, Caucasian parents believed the school discipline strategies were synchronized with those of the home; African American parents believed the school discipline strategies were markedly different from those practiced at home.

The remaining studies are all of large-scale populations. From these, a general profile of African American parents whose children attend Catholic schools emerges. In general, the African American parents of children who attend Catholic schools tend to be non-Catholic; they tend to be better educated than the general African American population; and, although their children may attend Catholic schools in poor areas, they tend not to be poor themselves (Benson et al., 1986).

The relationship between these family background variables and academic achievement for African Americans in Catholic schools is quite surprising. For example, among African American students enrolled in Catholic schools neither parental educational levels, occupational status, nor family income is related to academic achievement—a marked contrast from their relationship in public schools (Hoffer, Greeley & Coleman, 1985; Keith & Page, 1985; Marks & Lee, 1989). Family background factors are strongly influential in the academic achievement of public school students, particularly African American public school students. However, these same family background variables are less significantly related to achievement among African American students enrolled in Catholic schools. The phenomenon of background variables that influence outcomes in one context (public education) but not another (Catholic education) is known as the "Catholic school effect." This effect, interestingly, is greatest for African American students who are most at risk. In other words, the greatest gains in achievement are made by African Americans in Catholic schools whose family backgrounds are least conducive to success in the public school environment (Greeley, 1982; Lee & Stewart, 1989). The poorer and more at risk the minority student is, the greater the relative achievement gains in Catholic schools.

These findings on African American family background in Catholic schools raise questions. Are the potentially harmful effects of family background mediated in Catholic schools? If so, why and how? Does the economic and racial heterogeneity of Catholic schools (Coleman, Hoffer, & Kilgore, 1981) blur the social-class and race distinctions evident in public schools? Does the unity of parental commitment to Catholic education—across all social-class levels—encourage the perception of economic and social equality?

Student/Demographic Characteristics

The question of whether some individual characteristic or demographic element is related to achievement in Catholic schools has been explored since the 1970s. Table 1.4 examines a range of variables, including, but not limited to, the following: race, educational aspirations, intellectual ability, motivation to achieve, amount of television viewing and dating, gender, amount of time spent doing homework and talking to friends, and—more recently—religious affiliation, level of student vandalism, faith commitment, attendance in preschool or kindergarten, and global awareness. The propensity to give greater latitude to the measurement of a student's spiritual and religious commitment is a trend that can be seen in both Catholic-sponsored and secular research.

In this research, as in the research exploring family background, African American students in Catholic schools uniformly sustain higher levels of academic achievement than do African American students in public schools. For example, Keith and Page (1985), using the 1982 HSB data, found that educational aspirations had a stronger relationship to academic achievement among African Americans in Catholic schools than

TABLE 1.3. Studies of African American Achievement in Catholic Schools Using Family Background/Parental Characteristics

Year	Author(s)	Sample Characteristics	Achievement Measure	Family Background/Parental Characteristics Measure	Summary of Findings
1975	Miller & Kavanagh	All-female Catholic high school: 49% AA; 49% CA	Parental perceptions of achievement	Race/ethnicity	(1) AA and CA parents significantly supported quota systems, busing, integration and the active recruitment of minorities (2) AA parents felt daughters' achievement enhanced by attendance in integrated school; CA parents felt daughters' achievement diminished by attendance in integrated school (3) AA parents felt school discipline was not congruent with home discipline; CA parents felt school discipline was congruent with home discipline (4) Both AA and CA parents believed daughters gained skills in social interaction from attendance (5) 50% of AA parents supported integrated schooling in CS; 73% of CA parents opposed it
1982	Cibulka, O'Brien, & Zewe	54 inner-city CS elementary schools in major urban areas; student population 56% AA, 31% HS, and 8% CA	Iowa Test of Basic Skills (ITBS)	Parental income—majority of parents' incomes below poverty guidelines Parental education Parental religious affiliation	(1) AA parents had higher levels of education than AA national average (2) Majority of AA parents non-Catholic (3) Entering ITBS scores below national norms; after one year in CS, AA students averaged performance at or above grade level
1984	Byrk, Holland, Lee, & Carriedo	HSB 1982 plus data from 7 Catholic high schools (considered to be nonelite) and 13 feeder Catholic elementary schools	Reading Mathematics I Mathematics II	Academic emphasis throughout school Academic expectations Curriculum offerings Discipline policies and frequency of problems Emphasis on religion Sense of community Teacher beliefs Teacher commitment Parental involvement in school	(1) Emphasis on traditional academic curriculum (2) Common value system and developmental religion courses (3) High academic expectations for all students (4) Teachers personally involved with students and viewed teaching as a ministry (5) High levels of student engagement and few disruptive incidents (6) Schools selected by higher-income families for academic reasons; by lower-income families for religious reasons

1985	Hoffer, Greeley, & Coleman	HSB 1982	Reading Vocabulary Mathematics I Mathematics II Writing Science Civics	Family income Parental education Parental occupation Number of consecutive years of attendance at CS Father's aspirations for child Parental participation in school activities	(1) When family background variables are controlled, achievement among AACS students greater than among AAPS students (2) Effects of family background variables, particularly SES, lower in CS than in PS, particularly for AA students (3) Achievement scores for AA lower if no attendance at CS elementary school
1986	Benson et al.	106 Catholic high schools whose student bodies were at least 50% AA or HS and which reported that at least 10% of their students lived below the poverty line	1982 HSB scores in vocabulary, mathematics, and reading	Family SES Parental religious affiliation	(1) More than 33% of the AA students in these low-income schools were from nonpoor AA families (2) Statistically significant gains in vocabulary, reading, and mathematics, but not as great as HS or CA gains
1987	Lee	NAEP 1983-84; national sample of CS and PS students in grades 4, 8, and 11	Writing proficiency	Educational attainments of parent(s)	(1) Higher percentage of CS parents received more than high school education than PS parents (2) Both CS and PS students scored low on writing assessment measures
1989	Lee & Stewart	NAEP–NCEA sample of 1,900 3rd-, 7th-, and 11th-graders in CS	Mathematics Science	Educational attainments of parent(s) Working patterns of mother Family income	(1) Greatest achievement for AACS versus AAPS for children of parents with the least education (2) Mothers in both PS and CS work about equally, but proportion of working mothers highest for CS 11th-graders
1989	Marks & Lee	NAEP 1985–86: National sample of CS and PS students in grades 3, 7, and 11	Reading proficiency	Geographic region Parental education Maternal employment Parental academic expectations	(1) Achievement among AACS students less related to parental expectations and interest than among AAPS students (2) Achievement among AACS students less tied to levels of parental education than among AAPS students (3) Fewer mothers of CS students employed outside the home; however, higher achievement scores related to mothers who work part-time rather than full-time or unemployed

Note: The following abbreviations are used throughout the table: AA=African American HS=Hispanic CA=Caucasian CS=Catholic school PS=Public school

TABLE 1.4. Studies of African American Achievement in Catholic Schools Using Student/Demographic Characteristics

Year	Author(s)	Sample Characteristics	Achievement Measure	Individual/Demographic Characteristics Examined	Summary of Findings
1975	Miller & Kavanagh	All-female CS high school of 49% CA, 49% AA	Grades in school courses	Geographic region—urban Housing patterns SES—based on income	(1) AA parents felt attending integrated CS school increased achievement; CA parents believed it decreased achievement (2) AA parents did not believe attending CS aided family discipline; CS parents believed it did (3) AA and CA parents believed attendance aided in "social interaction skills"
1982	Cibulka, O'Brien, & Zewe	54 inner-city CS elementary schools	Iowa Test of Basic Skills	Race/ethnicity	(1) AACS achievement greater than AAPS
1985	Hoffer, Greeley, & Coleman	HSB 1982	Reading Vocabulary Mathematics I Mathematics II Writing Science Civics	Race/ethnicity Achievement motivation Television viewing Dating Talking to friends Driving in automobiles Amount of homework	(1) No significant differences among AA, HS, and CA on any individual behavioral characteristics (2) Effects of race lower in CS than in PS on achievement (3) Distance between AACS and AAPS achievement widened between sophomore and senior years (4) CS students spend significantly more time on homework regardless of race—significantly related to higher achievement
1985	Keith & Page	HSB 1982	Reading Mathematics I Mathematics II	Race/ethnicity Educational aspirations measured as intent to go to college Intellectual ability measured in verbal and nonverbal testing	(1) Effects of CS appear stronger for HS students than for AA (2) Ability measures strong predictor for achievement among AA student in CS (3) Aspiration had stronger effect on AA decision to attend CS than on HS
1986	Benson et al.	106 Catholic high schools whose student bodies were at least 50% AA or HS and which reported that at least 10% of their students lived below the poverty line	1982 HSB tests for vocabulary, mathematics, and reading	Race/ethnicity Religious affiliation Student vandalism Achievement motivation Faith commitment Global awareness Extracurricular activities Amount of television viewed Amount of homework done	(1) Vandalism lower in LI (low-income) CS than in MI (middle-income) CS (2) Failure to do homework higher in LICS than in MICS (3) AA in LICS place a higher emphasis on academics and discipline than CA or HS in LICS (4) AA in LICS made significantly greater gains than CA in LICS on faith commitment, religious commitment, and global awareness (5) Amount of homework completed, extracurricular activities, amount of television viewed, and achievement motivation significantly correlated to academic achievement gains, not to income or race

1987	Lee	Nationally representative sample of Catholic and public school students in grades 4, 8, and 11	1983-84 NAEP tests for writing proficiency	Race/ethnicity Geographic region	(1) CACS outscore AACS and HSCS at all three grade levels, but the CA advantage is significantly lower in CS than in PS (2) CAPS advantage is greater in writing
1989	Lee & Stewart	1,900 3rd-, 7th-, and 11th-graders in representative sample of CS	1983-84 NAEP tests for mathematics and science	Race/ethnicity Gender Geographic region Amount of homework done Amount of television viewed Presence of home computer	(1) Advantage for males in mathematics increases from grades 3 to 11 (2) Gaps between CACS and AACS significantly lessen from grades 3 to 11 (3) AACS > HSCS (4) CS students score higher than PS students in both mathematics and science in all geographic regions and residential areas, despite the disproportionate number of CS students in urban locations (5) 35% of PS students report doing < one hour of homework per day; 18% of CS students report doing < one hour of homework per day (6) Relationship between amount of television viewed and achievement is linear for 11th-graders in CS and PS, but effects are more damaging for PS students (7) In both kinds of schools, home computer ownership related positively to achievement
1989	Marks & Lee	NAEP data	Reading proficiency	Race/ethnicity Gender Achievement motivation Attendance in nursery, preschool, daycare, or kindergarten Amount of homework	(1) Reading proficiency advantage for females slight at grade 3 in both PS and CS; by grade 7, gap widens significantly, eventually narrowing in CS, but not in PS; female advantage persists in PS but not in CS (2) Scores higher for CA across all three grade levels, but gaps smaller in CS than PS (3) HSCS achievement greater than AACS (4) Attendance in early education related significantly to achievement among PS but not CS (5) CS students report significantly greater amounts of homework

Note: The following abbreviations are used throughout the table: AA=African American HS=Hispanic CA=Caucasian CS=Catholic school PS=Public school

among Hispanic students in the same schools or among African American students in public schools. In terms of behavioral measures shown to influence academic achievement (dating, television viewing, talking with friends, etc.), Hoffer, Greeley, and Coleman (1985)—again using the 1982 HSB data set—found no significant variations among Caucasian, African American, and Hispanic students enrolled in Catholic schools. Furthermore, behaviors thought to be antithetical to achievement (such as dating and television viewing) produced lower differences in achievement measures among Catholic school students of different races. These same behaviors in the public school domain, when held constant, produced significant differences in achievement among the three groups. Additionally, Catholic school students tended to spend significantly more time on homework than did public school students (regardless of race), and homework proved to be significantly related to achievement. Lee and Stewart (1989), using the 1983–84 NAEP tests for mathematics and science, confirmed these findings and also found that the gaps between achievement for the races—which widen in public schools as time passes—significantly decreased between grades 3 and 11 in Catholic schools.

An interesting study conducted by the National Catholic Education Association in 1985 (Benson et al., 1986) compared 1982 HSB scores for 106 low-income Catholic high schools (where the school population was at least 50% either African American or Hispanic and where at least 10% of the students were reported to live below the poverty line) with those of students in middle-income Catholic high schools. The findings were as follows:

1. The rates of school vandalism were higher at middle-income Catholic schools (predominantly nonminority) than at low-income Catholic (predominantly minority) schools.
2. African American students in low-income Catholic schools placed a greater emphasis on academics and discipline than did Caucasians or Hispanics in the same schools.
3. African American students in low-income Catholic schools showed significantly higher scores on measures of faith commitment, religious commitment, and global awareness than did Caucasians at the same schools.
4. Achievement was significantly correlated to amount of homework completed, number of extracurricular activities, the amount of television viewed, and achievement motivation. Achievement was not significantly correlated to either income or race.

These findings were confirmed in a later study by Marks and Lee (1989) using NAEP reading scores. Marks and Lee found that although

Caucasian reading scores were higher than African American scores in both public and Catholic schools, the gaps between scores for different groups were far less for students enrolled in Catholic schools. Furthermore, in public schools, attendance at preschool or kindergarten seemed related to increased reading scores. This relationship was not present for students in Catholic schools.

In general, the results from studies exploring student characteristics and demographic elements seem to contradict many of the relationships with academic achievement that are operational in public schools. African American students in Catholic schools do not score as well as their Caucasian counterparts, but they score significantly higher than African American students in public schools. Importantly, the deleterious effects of race, gender, and social class seem to be ameliorated, if not eradicated, in Catholic schools. This anomaly raises additional questions. Are there other, more subtle, individual characteristics that differentiate Catholic school from public school students? Does enrollment in a Catholic school, as an event, produce changes in the personality or character of the participating students? For example, does academic motivation or educational aspiration increase as a result of Catholic school enrollment? Are there elements of the school program or policies that intervene between traditionally negative family background and student characteristics, thus increasing the potential for academic achievement among African American students?

School Climate/Program and Teacher Characteristics

Because the traditional relationships between family background and student characteristics seem unrelated to achievement in Catholic schools, researchers have increasingly sought to measure ways school climate, school policies, teacher characteristics, and school procedures and programs may have intervened in the educational experiences of African American students. As mentioned earlier, this kind of research has received federal financial support, which may help to explain its popularity. Nonetheless, the kinds of school variables under examination have been quite extensive. These are listed in Table 1.2 and include quantifiable variables, such as expenditures per pupil, teacher and administrator membership in religious orders, placement of students in academic/vocational tracks, school size, and curriculum offerings, as well as variables difficult to quantify, such as morale, academic expectations, emphasis on religion, teacher beliefs, sense of community, sense of nurturing, and teacher commitment.

Results presented in Table 1.5 seem to suggest that Catholic schools certainly educate African American students differently than public

TABLE 1.5. Studies of African American Achievement in Catholic Schools Using School Climate/Program and Teacher Characteristics

Year	Author(s)	Sample Characteristics	Achievement Measure	School and Teacher Characteristics Examined	Summary of Findings
1982	Cibulka, O'Brien, & Zewe	54 inner-city CS elementary schools	Iowa Test of Basic Skills	Discipline policies and climate Attendance Sense of community Admissions criteria Teacher commitment Teacher salaries Teacher credentials Teacher experience Teacher membership in religious order	(1) AACS had fewer problems with discipline or attendance; 87% of schools had absentee rates of < 5% (2) 88% of teachers believed AACS well-behaved (3) 25% of schools had no admissions criteria; 80% accepted students with weak academic or behavioral backgrounds (4) Financial constraints caused inner-city CS to be closed five times faster than CS in other urban areas (5) Teachers of AACS had lower salaries; majority were laypeople (6) Almost all AACS teachers had an undergraduate degree, but not as many eligible for certification (7) AACS achievement scores higher than AAPS
1985	Hoffer, Greeley, & Coleman	HSB 1982	Reading Vocabulary Mathematics I Mathematics II Writing Science Civics	Academic track assignment Number of advanced courses Discipline problems and climate	(1) AACS enrolled in academic track had greater achievement gains than AAPS enrolled in academic track (2) AACS enrolled in nonacademic trace had greater achievement gains than AAPS enrolled in nonacademic track (3) AACS in nonacademic track significantly more likely to take advanced mathematics courses than AAPS in nonacademic track (4) Greater achievement gains for AACS than CACS (5) At least half of all achievement gains can be statistically explained by school climate and program variables (6) AACS placement in academic track more related to school requirements than to individual motivation
1985	Keith & Page	HSB 1982	Reading Mathematics I Mathematics II	Academic coursework taken by students, including advanced English, algebra I, algebra II, geometry, trigonometry, calculus, physics, and chemistry	Enrollment in these courses substantially reduced the effects of CS for AA students

1986	Benson et al.	106 Catholic schools whose student bodies were at least 50% AA or HS and which reported that at least 10% of their students lived below the poverty line	1982 HSB tests in vocabulary, mathematics, and reading	Teachers' membership in religious order Administrators' membership in religious order Religious beliefs and practices among staff Staff personal and social values School climate Academic expectations	(1) LI (low-income) CS requirements for attendance at religious retreats and services significantly higher than in MI (middle-income) CS (2) LICS administrators rated themselves significantly higher than non-LICS administrators on recruiting low-income students, sensitivity to racial and ethnic minorities, preparing for college, and offering remedial work (3) LICS faculty consider religious instruction and participation as important as academic instruction (4) LICS have higher expectations for academic excellence and doing homework and higher beliefs that students value learning than MICS
1989	Lee & Stewart	NCEA use of NAEP 1985-86 data	Science Mathematics	Placement in vocational/academic tracks Curriculum offerings in computer coursework, mathematics, and science	(1) Within-group comparisons of CS and PS students showed that in general education track, CS students outscored PS students in both areas, significantly higher in mathematics (2) Comparison of academic and vocational tracks showed less differentiation in CS than in PS (3) CS students significantly more likely to complete coursework in computer, science, and mathematics than national average (4) Although achievement scores among CS and PS students enrolled in mathematics and science courses not significantly different, the proportions of CS students enrolled in these courses significantly higher (5) Gaps between AACS and CACS students enrolled in advanced science and mathematics courses nonexistent (6) Significant differences between AACS and AAPS who enroll and complete advanced science and mathematics courses
1989	Marks & Lee	NAEP data	Reading proficiency	Curricular track Enrollment in English courses	(1) Significantly more CS students enrolled in academic track than PS (2) More CS students enrolled in advanced placement English than PS
1993	Bryk, Lee, & Holland	401 randomly selected HSB schools and 7 nationally representative Catholic high schools	Mathematics Science Reading	Curriculum offerings Discipline problems Placement in academic track Sense of community Teacher beliefs Expenditures per pupil School size Parental involvement	(1) AACS > AAPS and relationship strongest for AA most at risk (2) Strong sense of community linked to academic climate for achievement

Note: The following abbreviations are used throughout the table: AA=African American HS=Hispanic CA=Caucasian CS=Catholic school PS=Public school

schools and that these differences are salient in acceptance policies, curriculum, instruction, and school climate. For example, in a study of 54 inner-city Catholic schools, Cibulka and colleagues (1982) found that African Americans in Catholic schools had fewer problems with attendance and discipline than those in public schools. The Catholic schools had absentee rates of less than 5%. Teacher attitudes toward African American students seemed to be positive: Eighty-eight percent of teachers reported that the African American students they taught were very well behaved. Additionally, the assumption that the schools may indulge in a kind of elitist selectivity by accepting only well-behaved and intelligent students was unfounded. More than 25% of the schools had no admissions criteria, and more than 80% aggressively recruited students the public schools had diagnosed as academically or behaviorally problematic. Teachers' salaries in these Catholic schools were significantly lower than in the corresponding public schools, but student scores on the ITBS were significantly higher.

In a later study by Hoffer and colleagues (1985) using the 1982 HSB data to analyze African American and Caucasian scores on reading, vocabulary, mathematics, writing, science, and civics, African American achievement showed the same pattern. Specifically, African American students enrolled in academic tracks in Catholic schools showed greater levels of achievement than African American students enrolled in academic tracks in public schools. Similarly, African American students enrolled in vocational tracks in Catholic schools showed greater levels of achievement than African American students enrolled in vocational tracks in public schools. Hoffer and colleagues (1985) also found that African American students enrolled in vocational tracks were more likely to take advanced mathematics classes in Catholic schools than in public schools. Finally, achievement gains for African American students in Catholic schools were greater than for Caucasian students in Catholic schools. Hoffer and colleagues conclude that at least half of the achievement gains of African American students in Catholic schools can be explained by school climate and program variables and that these school-related variables supersede individual motivation in producing academic achievement.

Bryk and colleagues (1984), using the HSB data as well as extensive data gathered from seven Catholic high schools and thirteen elementary feeder schools, found that academic climate had a modest effect on academic achievement. A much greater effect stemmed from family background factors—particularly the degree of religious fervor of the parents, their social class, and their level of involvement in the Catholic school.

Like Greeley (1982), Bryk and colleagues conclude that social-class effects are significantly lessened in Catholic education. However, among the factors related to academic climate, they found the following:

1. Catholic high schools tend to emphasize a core academic curriculum, one that includes few or no "frills."
2. Teachers in Catholic high schools tend to believe that faith is a developmental process and structure their religious teaching accordingly. They tend to share a common value system that is congruent with (if not identical to) the major tenets of the Catholic faith.
3. Teachers tended to have high academic expectations for their students regardless of the student's family characteristics or background, yet their teaching styles were highly traditional, unremarkable, and structured.
4. A high level of student engagement in learning tended to be encouraged, and there were few incidents of disruptive behaviors among students.

In the National Catholic Education Association study of 106 low-income Catholic high schools containing large populations of poor and minority students (Benson et al., 1986), researchers found the following relationships between school-related variables and academic achievement:

1. In low-income Catholic schools (predominantly minority), the requirements that students attend religious retreats and religious services are significantly more stringent than in middle-income Catholic schools (predominantly nonminority).
2. Low-income Catholic school administrators rate themselves significantly higher than their middle-income school counterparts on sensitivity to racial and ethnic minorities, on recruiting minority students, and on offering meaningful remedial coursework.
3. Low-income Catholic school faculty tend to consider religious instruction and participation as important as academic instruction.
4. Low-income Catholic school faculties tend to have higher expectations for academic excellence and for doing homework than faculties in middle-income Catholic schools. Additionally, faculties in low-income Catholic schools tend to believe that students value learning far more than do faculties in middle-income Catholic schools.

Taken together, this research seems to suggest that Catholic schools educate low-income minority students differently than public schools and differently than middle-income Catholic schools, particularly in their treatment of African American students. Some researchers have suggested that because Catholic schools lack the financial resources available to public education, the students who enroll in Catholic schools enjoy an unintended advantage over their public school cohorts. For example, a small Catholic high school may not have the financial resources to maintain both a vocational curriculum and academic curriculum; students enrolled in that school may therefore be forced to take advanced mathematics and literature courses simply because nothing else is available. Other aspects of school uniformity—such as wearing uniforms and attending religious retreats together—have also been cited as contributing to a school climate that supersedes family and individual characteristics. Interestingly, although the numbers of nuns, priests, and brothers who are members of teaching orders have declined sharply in recent years, the percentage of nuns, priests, and brothers on Catholic school faculties has remained higher in low-income Catholic schools than in any other segment of Catholic education.

SUMMARY OF RESEARCH AND RECOMMENDATIONS FOR FURTHER RESEARCH

As a whole, this research seems to provide evidence of three ways in which Catholic schools function in the lives of African American students enrolled in them. First, family background variables such as income, parental educational levels, and parental educational aspirations seem less important in the achievement gains of African American students in Catholic schools than in public schools. Second, individual characteristics such as intelligence, achievement motivation, gender, religious affiliation, and race seem similarly less related to African American academic achievement in Catholic schools. Finally, several school-related variables, perhaps acting in concert, seem to contribute significantly to the academic achievement of African American students in Catholic schools.

The need for further research into the effects of Catholic schooling is clear, particularly research that can offer further explanations concerning the achievement of African American students enrolled in Catholic schools. The study of African Americans in Catholic schools has been conducted as a secondary topic; that is, findings on African Americans are generated largely a subset of a larger (predominantly Caucasian) population. Hence studies that focus on African Americans as a primary population would provide a means of exploring the unique adaptations made by African Americans who are educated in Catholic schools. This research, conducted in the context of the separatist cultural history of Catholic education in the United States, could help explain why Catholic schools in the United States seem to create a culturally congruent context for African Americans that enhances their academic achievement. Additionally, studies that utilize and test previous research on African Americans may aid in substantiating or creating theories that explain achievement. Finally, different research designs are needed to broaden our means of capturing the processes and outcomes of Catholic education, particularly the Catholic education of African American children.

REFERENCES

Benson, P. L., Yeager, R. J., Guerra, M. J., & Manno, B. V. (1986). *Catholic high schools: Their impact on low-income students.* Washington, DC: National Catholic Educational Association.

Bredeweg, F. H. (1985). United States Catholic elementary and secondary schools 1984–85. In M. Mahar (Ed.), NCEA/*Ganley's Catholic schools in America, 1985* (13th ed.). Montrose, CO: Fisher.

Bryk, A., Holland, P., Lee, V., & Carriedo, R. (1984). *Effective Catholic schools: An exploration.* Washington, DC: National Catholic Educational Association.

Bryk, A., Lee, V., & Holland, P. (1993). *Catholic schools and the common good.* Cambridge, MA: Harvard University Press.

Cibulka, J. G., O'Brien, T. J., & Zewe, D. (1982). *Inner-city private elementary schools.* Milwaukee: Marquette University Press.

Coleman, J. S. (1981). Quality and equality in American education: Public and Catholic schools. *Phi Delta Kappan, 62,* 159–164.

Coleman, J. S., & Hoffer, T. (1987). *Public and private high schools.* New York: Basic Books.

Coleman, J. S., Hoffer, T., & Kilgore, S. (1981). *Public and private schools* (Final report to the National Center for Education Statistics, Contract No. 300–78–0208). Chicago: National Opinion Research Center.

Coleman, J., Hoffer, T., & Kilgore, S. (1982). *High school achievement: Public, Catholic, and private schools compared.* New York: Basic Books.

Condon, H. C. (1984). *High School and Beyond tabulation: Type of schools attended by 1980 high school sophomores from grades 1–12.* Washington, DC: National Center for Education Statistics.

Convey, J. J. (1989). Catholic schools, Research on. In B. Marthaler (Ed.), *The New Catholic Encyclopedia, 18,* 73–78. Palatine, IL: Jack Heraty & Associates.

Cremin, L. A. (1988). *American education: The colonial experience.* New York: Basic Books.

Dolan, J. P. (1981). *The immigrant church: New York's Irish and German Catholics: A history of the Roman Catholic community in the United States*. New York: Oxford University Press.

Dolan, J. P. (1985). *The American Catholic experience*. Garden City, NY: Doubleday.

Ellis, J. T. (1956). *American Catholics and the intellectual life*. Chicago: Heritage Foundation.

Greeley, A. M. (1982). *Catholic high schools and minority students*. New Brunswick, NJ: Transaction Books.

Greeley, A. M., & Rossi, P. B. (1966). *The education of Catholic Americans*. Chicago: Aldine.

Hoffer, T., Greeley, A. M., & Coleman, J. S. (1985). Achievement growth in public and Catholic schools. *Sociology of Education, 58*(4), 74–79.

Hunt, T. C., & Kunkel, N. M. (1988). Catholic schools: The nation's largest alternative school system. *New Catholic World, 6*, 277–310.

Keith, T. Z., & Page, E. B. (1985). Do Catholic schools really improve minority achievement? *American Educational Research Journal, 22*, 337–349.

Kraushaar, O. F. (1972). *American nonpublic schools: Patterns of diversity*. Baltimore: Johns Hopkins University Press.

Lazerson, M. (1977). Understanding American Catholic educational history. *History of Education Quarterly, 17*, 297–317.

Lee, V. E. (1987). *1983–84 National Assessment of Educational Progress writing proficiency: Catholic school results and national averages*. Washington, DC: National Catholic Educational Association.

Lee, V. E., & Stewart, C. (1989). *National Assessment of Educational Progress proficiency in mathematics and science 1985–86: Catholic and public schools compared*. Washington, DC: National Catholic Educational Association.

Madaus, G. F., & Linnan, R. (1973). The outcome of Catholic education. *School Review, 81*(2), 207–232.

Marks, H. M., & Lee, V. E. (1989). *National Assessment of Educational Progress proficiency in reading: 1985–86. Catholic and public schools compared. Final Report 1989*. Washington, DC: National Catholic Educational Association.

Miller, S. I., & Kavanagh, J. (1975). Catholic school integration and social policy: A case study. *Journal of Negro Education, 44*(4), 482–491.

O'Dea, T. F. (1958). *The American Catholic dilemma: An inquiry into the intellectual life*. New York: Shedd & Ward.

Perko, F. M. (1987). Catholics and their schools from a culturalist perspective. *New Catholic World, 6*, 124–129.

Sanders, J. W. (1977). *The education of an urban minority: Catholics in Chicago, 1833–1865*. New York: Oxford University Press.

Vitullo-Martin, T. (1979). *Catholic inner-city schools: The future*. Washington, DC: United States Catholic Conference.

CHAPTER 2

First Came the School: Catholic Evangelization Among African Americans in the United States, 1827 to the Present

V. P. Franklin

The relationship of the Roman Catholic Church to African Americans in the United States has been distinctive from the early nineteenth century to the present. One of the most distinctive elements historically was the fact that Black Catholic schools were more important in the evangelization of the African American population than were Catholic missionary activities. In the eighteenth and nineteeth centuries, when Catholic missionaries encountered the native American Indian population in North America, religious conversions were often brought about through evangelization and the opening of missionary schools. However, when Catholic missionaries began working among enslaved Africans in the southern colonies and states during the same time period, there were very few attempts made to provide religious training or schooling. One reason for the failure to provide religious instruction was the existence of legislation in those areas that prohibited teaching slaves to read and write. While Catholic missionaries became well known for their evangelical campaigns among and in defense of the Native American population in the wake of European conquests and domination, they were less likely to evangelize or educate the enslaved Africans in the New World and more likely to participate in Black exploitation and oppression (Buetow, 1971; Miller, 1983).

EDUCATION AND EVANGELIZATION

Many Catholic religious orders in antebellum America owned slaves, and while there were some attempts made at religious instruction, there is little evidence that the Jesuits in Maryland, the Sulpicians, Sisters of Charity, and Sisters of Loretto in Kentucky, or the Capuchins in Louisiana were involved in systematic efforts to bring about religious conversions among enslaved Africans (Curran, 1983). Cyprian Davis (1990) in *The History of Black Catholics in the United States* noted that during the antebellum era pronouncements were issued by Catholic bishops reminding Catholic slaveowners of "their duty to furnish their slaves with opportunities for being well instructed, and for practicing their religion," but actual efforts to provide religious training for enslaved Africans were few and far between (p. 44).

Before the Civil War, Catholic evangelization through the provision of schooling for African Americans was aimed primarily at the free Black population in northern and southern cities. It is believed that the first school opened by Roman Catholics for African Americans was located in Washington, D.C. In 1827 Maria Becraft opened a school for free Black girls in the Holy Trinity Church in Georgetown (Davis, 1990). With the founding of the Oblate Sisters of Providence, the first order of Black nuns in the United States, St. Frances Academy for Colored Girls was opened for free blacks in Baltimore in June 1828. During the antebellum period the Oblate Sisters opened three other schools in the city—St. Frances Boys School in 1852 and St. Michael's and St. Joseph's in 1857, the latter being the first black parish school. During and immediately after the Civil War, the Oblate Sisters opened other schools for Black children, including St. Peter Claver School in Philadelphia and St. Joseph School in New Orleans, and sponsored "colored orphan asylums" in Baltimore and New Orleans that provided some educational programs (Gerdes, 1988; Traxler, 1969).

The outbreak of the Civil War and the subsequent emancipation of the slaves served as the impetus for launching the freedmen's aid movement, or Christian Reconstruction. Secular and religious philanthropic associations were formed throughout the North for the purpose of providing food, clothing, medicine, and schooling to the tens of thousands of former slaves gathering behind Union lines. Male and female, Black and white teachers and missionaries were sent into the South to assist the freedpeople in their transition from slavery to freedom (Richardson, 1986).

During the war years it was primarily the schools and orphanages opened by the Oblate Sisters in Baltimore and New Orleans that represented the Roman Catholic response to emancipation, and it was not until October 1866 at the Second Plenary Council of Baltimore that the American Catholic episcopate addressed the issue of the evangelization of the former slaves. In their pastoral letter the bishops acknowledged that "a new and most extensive field of charity and devotedness has been opened to us by the immense slave population of the South," but they also expressed some reservations and made it clear that they would have preferred "a more gradual system of emancipation" because of the "evils which must necessarily attend upon the sudden liberation of so large a multitude, with their peculiar dispositions and habits" (Davis, 1990, p. 122). In his comments on the pastoral letter, Cyprian Davis noted that the sentiments expressed "were scarcely magnanimous or generous" and revealed "the sort of barriers that black Catholics had to face within their own church for the rest of the century" (p. 121).

Historian Ronald Butchart (1980), in a survey of educational programs provided for the freedpeople during the Reconstruction period, concluded that "although the [Catholic] church's Second Plenary Council, held at Baltimore in 1866, had announced intentions to extend its ministry to the freedmen, that commitment carried as much weight as similar pronouncements by southern Protestants" (p. 39). Butchart mentioned the Black Catholic schools opened in Baltimore, Savannah, St. Augustine, and other southern cities. However, given the hundreds of thousands of southern Blacks in need of schooling, Butchart came to the same conclusions as later researchers that the Catholic response to emancipation was minimal and ultimately insignificant (Misch, 1974).

When four Mill Hill missionary priests were sent from England to the United States in 1871 to evangelize specifically among African Americans, they decided to establish a school for Black children at the St. Francis Xavier Church in Baltimore (Ochs, 1990). In December 1878, Father John Slattery was made rector of St. Francis Xavier Church, and he soon became convinced that the only way to increase the number of African American conversions to Catholicism was through the development of a Black clergy. And the best way to gain African American vocations to the priesthood would be through the opening of Black Catholic schools. The Third Plenary Council of Roman Catholic Bishops was held in Baltimore in 1884, and although the "Commission for Catholic Missions Among Indians and Colored People" was created, the bishops failed to address the issue of Black vocations to the priesthood. However, Father Slattery kept up his campaign for the training of Black priests and was instrumental in the recruitment of several African Americans to the priesthood. When St. Joseph's Seminary was opened by the Mill Hill Fathers in Baltimore in 1888, Father Slattery saw to it that Black students were admitted on a basis of equality. Unfortunately, only a handful of African Americans enrolled at St. Joseph's during those early years, further emphasizing the need for elementary and secondary schools for Black Catholics to encourage religious vocations (Davis, 1990; Ochs, 1990).

One of the major reasons why Catholic officials failed to respond to Father Slattery's crusade for African American clergy was that the Church had become preoccupied with the burgeoning immigrant population entering the United States and was in need of churches, schools, priests, and nuns to maintain newcomers' Catholic faith in the Protestant-dominated environment. Between 1870 and 1900 the number of Catholics in the United States increased from 4,504,000 to 12,041,000, due primarily to the New Immigration (Franklin, 1981). Thus evangelization among African Americans was not nearly as important as the maintenance of the faith among those who were already Catholic. However, during this same period the Black Catholic laity decided to address the issue of evangelization and education in a series of five Colored Catholic Congresses, held between 1889 and 1894. Under the leadership of Daniel Rudd, Lincoln Valle, and Frederick McGhee, Black Catholics from throughout the country not only met and decried the racial discrimination practiced by white Catholics, but pledged themselves to the support of Catholic schools for Black children (Davis, 1990; Spalding, 1969).

Despite the efforts of the Black Catholic laity and committed white priests such as Father John Slattery, there was no significant increase in the number of Black Catholic schools or Black Catholic priests between 1895 and 1918. Facing increasing opposition from southern bishops to the assignment of Black priests to their dioceses, even the Josephites began to reject Black applicants to St. Joseph Seminary. In a 1914 report prepared by the representative of the Roman Curia sent to the United States to evaluate the situation, Archbishop Giovanni Bonzano concluded that at the most a thousand African Americans were converted to Catholicism each year between 1900 and 1914, but the number who left the church annually was very likely even greater (Davis, 1990, p. 206).

BLACK CATHOLIC LAITY AND EDUCATION

The Black Catholic laity remained concerned about the declining numbers of Black Catholics in the United States, and in 1917 Dr. Thomas Wyatt Turner, a biology professor at Howard University and member of St. Augustine Church in Washington, D. C., called a meeting at his home to discuss these problems. The Committee Against the Extension of Race Prejudice in the Church grew out of these meetings, and according to historian Marilyn W. Nickels, "the members wrote letters to the hierarchy about discriminatory practices in the Church, the lack of proper educational facilities for black children or opportunities for higher education, and the urgent need of a black priesthood" (Nickels, 1988, p. 3).

By 1919 the group had expanded and become known as the Committee for the Advancement of Colored Catholics, with 25 members and branches in Baltimore and Washington, D. C. The Committee's most important activity in the immediate postwar period was to challenge the changes in the Josephites' policy of restricting the number of African Americans admitted to its seminaries for training in the priesthood. Stephen J. Ochs (1990), *Desegregating the Altar: The Josephites and the Struggle for Black Priests, 1871–1960,* presented a detailed examination of the Committee's efforts to expose these discriminatory practices, concluding that although there was little change in the Josephite policy between 1919 and 1924, "the persistence of black Catholics kept the issue of black priests before church authorities, both in the United States and Rome. As a result, even as Turner and his allies battled [Louis] Pastorelli [the Josephite superior general], two missionary societies—the Society of the Divine Word and the Society of African Missions—with significant support from the Holy See, moved to establish seminaries that would educate black men for the priesthood" (Ochs, 1990, p. 245).

Encouraged by its success in influencing Church officials, the Committee for the Advancement of Colored Catholics in 1925 called for a national meeting of what soon became the Federated Colored Catholics of the United States. Meeting at St. Augustine Church in Washington, D.C., in December 1925, delegates from Philadelphia, Chicago, and other northern cities met and elected officers, made arrangements to develop a permanent constitution, and resolved to support the Cardinal Gibbons Institute, recently opened in Ridge, Maryland, as a secondary school for Black Catholic youth. John LaFarge, a Jesuit priest and the guiding force behind the opening of the Cardinal Gibbons Institute, was very supportive of the Federated Colored Catholics' activities in its early years (Nickels, 1988; Phelps, 1988; Portier, 1986).

Father LaFarge had been impressed by the educational work of Booker T. Washington in Alabama and envisioned the Gibbons Institute as a "Catholic Tuskegee." Washington's educational program, supported by northern industrial philanthropists, sought to provide the separate Black public school systems with a cadre of conservative teachers who specialized in industrial education. At Cardinal Gibbons Institute, under the leadership of Black educators Victor and Constance Daniel, students were provided vocational and agricultural training, and educational programs were offered to Black farmers in the surrounding communities in southern Maryland. Initially, the school received financial support from the General Education Board, the Julius Rosenwald Fund, the state of Maryland, and the American Catholic Home Mission Board. With the coming of the Great Depression in 1929, however, the Institute began experiencing financial problems, and efforts were made to raise money through the establishment of a public relations office in New York City. Unfortunately, the school's debts continued to increase, and in December 1933 it was forced to close. Eventually, the land and buildings were sold to the local diocese, which opened a Black secondary school on the site in 1936 (LaFarge, 1954; Nickels, 1988).

The closing of Cardinal Gibbons Institute in 1933 coincided with a split in the Federated Colored Catholics, in which Father LaFarge had become involved. Whereas Father LaFarge and his Jesuit colleague William Markoe had championed the commitment to the development of a Black clergy in the United States to increase evangelization among African Americans, the two priests also believed that the Federated Colored Catholics should move more quickly in the direction of "interracial activities" within the Catholic Church. Dr. Turner and the original founders of the organization saw its purpose as primarily self-determinist—to serve as a vehicle for developing unity and cooperation among Black Catholics and as their voice in Catholic circles. While the Black Catholics welcomed the support of white clergy and laity, they objected to the white priests' attempts to dominate the organization and to define its purposes. The conflict led to a split among the membership in 1933 and the creation of the National Catholic Interracial Federation. The Federated Colored Catholics continued in existence in a much weakened form until the early 1960s (Nickels, 1988).

Marilyn W. Nickels in her detailed account of the conflict concluded that this controversy arose over the attempts of Black Catholics to create an "independent authority" within a "hierarchical Church." Cyprian Davis, however, viewed Dr. Turner and his associates as part of "a long line of black protest leaders. They were heirs of the black Catholic congress movement of the 1890s and forerunners of the civil rights movement and the black Catholic movement that evolved from it in the 1960s." These Black Catholic leaders represented a "tradition of lay leadership that characterized the history of the black Catholic community" (Davis, 1990, p. 229; Franklin, 1992). More important, this historical controversy is important to our understanding of Catholic educational activities among African Americans.

From the beginning, the Federated Colored Catholics made clear their support for the opening of Black Catholic schools, which they saw as extremely important for the maintenance of the faith among Black Catholics from one generation to the next. However, the greater part of the group's energies was devoted to exposing and denouncing racial discrimination within Catholic institutions. For example, one of the major preoccupations of the Federated Colored Catholics in the 1920s and early

1930s was the unsuccessful campaign aimed at the Church hierarchy to allow African Americans to enroll at Catholic University in Washington, D.C. Indeed, one reason why Xavier Academy, the Black Catholic secondary school opened in New Orleans in 1914 through the financial support of Blessed Katherine Drexel, became a collegiate institution in the early 1930s was because the Catholic hierarchy refused to change the discriminatory admissions policies at Catholic colleges and universities across the country. With the creation of "Xavier University" as a Black Catholic institution of higher education, there was less pressure on Catholic college and university administrators to allow African Americans to enroll in their institutions, and the desegregation of Catholic higher education in the United States would not take place until after World War II (St. John, 1977).

CATHOLIC SCHOOLS AND BLACK CATHOLIC IDENTITY

The practice of maintaining separate Black Catholic schools was not confined to the Jim Crow South in the first half of the twentieth century; it was also official policy in the large Catholic dioceses in the North. And, as was the case in the South, Black Catholic schools in northern cities served as a major vehicle for spreading the Catholic faith among African Americans. For example, in 1930 Chicago had the largest parochial school system in the country, with more than 145,000 pupils enrolled in its 235 parish schools. Throughout the 1930s Archbishop George Mundelein enforced a policy of segregation in the Catholic elementary schools in the city. According to historian James Sanders, although African Americans were allowed to attend Mass at any of the city's Catholic churches, Black children were enrolled only at St. Elizabeth Parish School on the Southside. When confronted by Black Catholic parents about this practice in 1930, Archbishop Mundelein made his position clear: "Nothing will be accomplished for the evangelization of the colored in Chicago by scattering them among the whites in our churches and schools, but rather by keeping them by themselves and concentrating the work for them in churches and schools restricted to them" (quoted in Sanders, 1977, p. 213).

Despite the enforced segregation, Church officials believed that the Black Catholic schools "have proved to be the best convert makers." A 1938 report estimated that "since 1930 the Negro Catholic population of Chicago has doubled. There are now some 16,000 colored Catholics in the Archdiocese" (Sanders, 1977, pp. 215–216). During World War II there was a huge migration of southern Blacks to Chicago, and, following a number of protests by Black Catholics, the archdiocese in 1945 opened the doors of all parish schools to African Americans (Sanders, 1977). Sociologists St. Clair Drake and Horace Cayton in their important work, *Black Metropolis: A Study of Negro Life in a Northern City,* published in 1945, reported that "at the present time Negroes are allowed to join the nearest parish church and to send their children to the parish school." They believed that "one of the primary attractions of the Catholic Church is its educational institutions. . . . Many parents felt that the parochial school offered a more thorough education in a quieter atmosphere and personal attention" (Drake & Cayton, 1945, pp. 414–416). However, by the end of the 1940s the shift in official policy had resulted not in the desegregation of Catholic elementary schools in Chicago but in an increase in the number of all-Black or predominantly Black Catholic schools (Sanders, 1977).

Several researchers have suggested that one of the primary reasons African Americans joined the Catholic Church in the post–World War II era was the availability of low-cost, high-quality education in Catholic parish schools, particularly in deteriorating inner-city neighborhoods. Southern migrants arriving in northern and western cities found that the local public schools were often overcrowded, understaffed, and poorly equipped. The Catholic parish schools, however, represented an inexpensive alternative to this situation, and many working- and middle-class Black parents, Catholic and non-Catholic alike, enrolled their children (Cibulka, 1988; Franklin & McDonald, 1988).

While educational researchers agree that there was a significant increase in the number of African American children enrolled in Catholic elementary schools from 1930 to 1960 in both the North and the South, differences of opinion exist over whether or not these institutions helped to create and maintain a positive "Black Catholic identity." In a recent study, *Black and Catholic in Savannah, Georgia,* anthropologist Gary Wray McDonogh (1993) examined the records at the three separate black Catholic elementary schools in 1958–59, before the official desegregation of Catholic education in the South. McDonogh found that of the 175 students enrolled in St. Anthony's Parish School, only 69 were Catholic. At Most Pure Heart of Mary School, there were only 114 Catholics out of a total of 333 students, and at Saint Benedict's only 76 of the 326 students were Catholic. It was only in the all-Black Saint Pius High School that a majority of the students, 83 out of 119, were Catholic in 1959. Although the majority of the students enrolled in these schools considered themselves non-Catholic, McDonogh argued that these schools were important in the development of a distinct "black Catholic identity" even among the non-Catholic students. While McDonogh (1993) found that the Catholic educational undertaking in Savannah was fraught with cultural contradictions and ambivalence, "despite or perhaps because of this ambivalence, the school emerged as a part of the community, where the classroom was intrinsically bound to the family, the neighborhood, and the parish" (p. 119).

The white nuns who taught in Savannah's Black Catholic schools represented a kind of "mystical presence," and the fact that they were teachers in all-Black institutions made them "sociologically Black." The course of study in Savannah's Black Catholic schools was academic, and no "manual" or "industrial" education classes were offered. This made the Catholic schools more attractive to the upwardly mobile, middle- and working-class Black families. Catechism and religion were a basic part of the curriculum and had the effect of converting the students, if not the parents, to Catholicism. However, parents who took religious classes and converted to Catholicism were charged less tuition than nonconverts. Strict discipline was enforced through the use of corporal punishment, of which most parents approved. And the school uniforms became "a badge of Catholic distinctiveness in the city" (McDonogh, 1993, p. 112).

Historian Michael McNally (1987) examined Black and white parish schools in cities in the southeastern United States and concluded that "black Catholic schools were of much more significance [in bringing about religious conversions] than black parishes," mainly because "black Catholic churches reached only the small numbers of black Catholics of the region, whereas schools, whose student body was mostly Protestant, reached a broader spectrum of the black population" (p. 183). As was the case with Gary McDonogh, McNally suggested that these Black Catholic schools were a positive element because they "operated locally right within their own community" and the quality of the schooling provided was generally better than that found in the segregated public schools. However, McNally argued that these Black schools did not serve the same functions as did Catholic schools for other ethnic groups in the region and did not contribute to the development of a positive Black self-concept.

> Unlike the German or Irish parish schools, the teachers in black Catholic schools were often not from the same ethnic background as their students, that is, not black. Unlike the student population of the European ethnic schools, most students in African Catholic schools were Protestant. Unlike the other Catholic ethnic schools, which were designed to preserve language, culture and ethnic pride, black Catholic schools exposed their pupils to the prevailing white American culture and tradition, including, sadly, racism. . . . The black Catholic schools did not communicate to their students a very positive self-image or a strong sense of self-worth, or pride in one's ethnic heritage, all of which are so necessary in the fulfillment of one's human potential. (McNally, 1987, pp. 182–183)

The findings of other researchers of the Black experience in Catholic schools, however, have been somewhat different and tend to support the conclusions reached by McDonogh. For example, when we examine the history and development of the 75 Black Catholic elementary and secondary schools opened in the nineteenth and twentieth centuries by the Oblate Sisters of Providence, the Sisters of the Holy Family, and the Franciscan Handmaidens of Mary, we find that both the students and teachers were African American. Theresa A. Rector, in her examination of the history and development of the schools founded by Black women's religious orders, found that "with few exceptions, the Sisters who have manned these schools have been a tremendous source of inspiration for those with whom they came in contact. They have selflessly served humanity wherever the need arose. They have served as role models for the young impressionable girls in their schools, as mothers for the orphaned, as nurses and doctors for the sick. In the area of education they have sought to maintain schools of the highest academic quality in which youths are taught sound values to guide them throughout adulthood" (Rector, 1982, pp. 239–240).

I examined the separate Black public and Catholic schools in Philadelphia during the first half of the twentieth century and also found that the Black Catholic schools often maintained strong ties to the local Black communities and often served as social centers and meeting places for a number of Black groups and organizations. Before the 1940s, all the teachers and principals in the separate Black public schools in Philadelphia were African Americans. However, in the Black Catholic schools virtually all the nuns and teachers were white, but these predominantly Black Catholic institutions celebrated African American cultural events, such as Negro History Week, and offered a wide array of educational programs and conferences aimed at the entire Black community (Franklin, 1979, 1983).

Similar activities were found in the Black Catholic schools in Savannah, Georgia. Although initially the "foreign Catholic missionaries" who established schools for Blacks in Savannah were unaware of the culturally defined educational values that existed in the African American community, eventually the white priests and nuns were able to develop grassroots support for their educational endeavors. According to Gary McDonogh (1993):

> Once the Catholic system took a solid foundation, a new sense of education emerged, which drew on the culture of the marked group as much as the ideals of the white missionaries. This education linked parish and school, classroom and community in its goals and practice. It became the foundation of the modern black and Catholic community, which made active contribu-

> tions to the school, yet this creation could still be dominated by white society. The agony felt when white administrators closed black schools showed the continuing conflict between blacks and whites embedded in urban and religious culture. These events appear more tragic since everyone, apparently, tried to meet their publicly professed Christian ideals, yet all were caught by contradictions in their society and culture. (p. 139)

The major increase in expenses for urban Catholic schools, which ultimately led to numerous school closings in poor and working-class Black neighborhoods, came from the need to provide competitive salaries to the increasing numbers of lay teachers. Before the 1960s the vast majority of the teachers in urban Catholic schools were nuns, priests, and brothers who were supported by their religious orders. The salaries paid to these teachers were quite low, and this allowed Catholic school officials to keep tuition costs lower than in nonreligious private schools. With the decline in religious vocations beginning in the 1960s, more and more lay teachers were hired by Catholic school administrators, which drove up the costs. When the tuition was raised to meet the new expenses, enrollments declined, and many Catholic parish schools were consolidated and closed (Cibulka, 1988).

To a much greater extent than was the case in the North, in Savannah and other southern cities the closings of the Black Catholic schools were dictated by legal mandates and legislative directives. For example, in Savannah the major thrust behind the closing of separate Black Catholic schools was the need to bring about the official desegregation of Catholic educational institutions. On the other hand, in many northern and western cities the closing of Catholic schools in Black neighborhoods was the result of declining enrollments and revenues, and increasing expenses (Franklin & McDonald, 1988). However, in both the North and the South the protests launched by Black Catholics over the closing of elementary and secondary schools in Black neighborhoods made it clear that these educational institutions were considered an important part of the African American cultural heritage in that area. As one student noted at the closing of the all-Black St. Pius High School in Savannah in 1971: "It is the only institution that we had been able to hold onto and say it's ours. Various people who hold leadership positions do so because of Saint Pius" (quoted in McDonogh, 1993, p. 122).

URBAN CATHOLIC SCHOOLS AND BLACK ACADEMIC ACHIEVEMENT

While there has been little or no systematic examination of the occupational status and career patterns for Black Catholic school graduates in general, there have been a number of studies of the academic achievement levels attained by African American and other ethnic minority students enrolled in urban Catholic schools. Andrew Greeley, in a 1980 study of Black and Hispanic students enrolled in Catholic secondary schools, found achievement levels much higher than those for minority students in public high schools, even when family background characteristics, such as parental education and income, were taken into account (Greeley, 1980). Thomas Z. Keith looked at the achievement test scores of Black and Hispanic high school seniors in the first wave of the (1982) High School and Beyond longitudinal study who were enrolled in Catholic and public schools. Keith found that when measures of student ability, such as reading comprehension skills, were taken into account, the apparent positive effect of Catholic schools was reduced, though still meaningful. Keith suggested that greater homework demands in the Catholic schools may partially account for the differences in the effects of schooling on Black and Hispanic high school students (Keith, 1982; Keith & Page, 1985).

With regard to African Americans and other minority students in Catholic elementary schools, the findings were similar. The most comprehensive study was commissioned in 1978 by the Catholic League for Religious and Civil Rights. This study included 54 private, mostly Catholic, schools in which Blacks accounted for 56% of the enrollment, Hispanics 31%, and whites 8%. All the schools charged tuition, averaging $400 per year, and the families had an average income of $15,000 per year, with 15% of the families earning less than $5,000 in 1978. These particular families, however, were noticeably similar in public educational background and Protestant religious affiliation with their neighbors. However, one important factor distinguished the parents in these families: "their desire for high quality education." According to one report, "analyses of the responses of parents showed that this factor outweighed all others, including religious beliefs." Although the schools were "overwhelmingly Catholic" in affiliation, "nearly one-third (31%) of the students were Protestant and 2% listed themselves as having no church affiliation. Among Black students, the proportion of non-Catholics was even higher; 53% of all Black students reported that they were Protestant" (Blum, 1985, pp. 643–644; Slaughter & Schneider, 1986).

On a number of significant nonacademic measures, including frequency of student discipline and attendance problems and parent–teacher relations, these private Catholic schools appeared to be serving their minority clientele quite well. There were far fewer student discipline problems in the Catholic schools, and parent–teacher relations were close and cooperative. This was understandable since these parents had invested great amounts of time and money in the decision to enroll their children in private school and were generally attentive to their investment. Teachers and administrators of urban Black Catholic parish schools often faced enormous financial stresses, including frequent vandalism, high insurance premiums, and economic insecurities among the students. Oftentimes, these dedicated educators were sustained primarily by the spiritual support of working- and middle-class Black parents committed to maintaining high-quality educational programs for their children (Franklin & McDonald, 1988; National Office of Black Catholics [NOBC], 1976).

There seems to be much evidence that the closing of Catholic schools in predominantly Black urban areas deprives Black parents and children, Catholic and non-Catholic, of an important educational alternative that has produced high levels of academic achievement among African American children. However, the controversy over the closing of Catholic schools in urban Black neighborhoods touched off another debate within Catholic circles about whether or not Catholic money and resources should be used for the training of non-Catholic children. Whereas the church's pragmatists often pointed out that many inner-city parish schools had become a drain on the diocese's financial resources, many Black Catholic leaders saw these schools as important outposts for attracting Black converts and argued that these schools should be considered part of the Catholic Church's mission to the Black community (NOBC, 1976; Schillo, 1980; Vitullo-Martin, 1979).

The history of Black Catholic schools in the United States reveals that in both the North and the South the majority of students enrolled were often non-Catholic. Given this historical reality, the contemporary suggestion that Catholic resources should not be used to provide schooling for Black non-Catholics has little or no support. In the past Black Catholic schools have been the most important element in the evangelization of the African American population in the United States and remain significant for the maintenance of the faith among Black Catholics. The abandonment of these schools has come to symbolize a lack of interest among Catholic officials in further African American conversions. Black and white Catholics interested in expanding the role and influence of Catholicism among African Americans must recognize that the closing of Catholic schools in Black neighborhoods threatens the maintenance and expansion of Catholicism within the largest and most important minority community in the United States.

REFERENCES

Blum, V. C. (1985). Private elementary education in the inner city. *Phi Delta Kappan, 66,* 643–646.

Buetow, H. A. (1971). The underprivileged and Roman Catholic education. *The Journal of Negro Education, 40,* 373–389.

Butchart, R. E. (1980). *Northern schools, southern blacks, and reconstruction: freedmen's education, 1862–1875.* Westport, CT: Greenwood.

Cibulka, J. G. (1988). Catholic school closings: Efficiency, responsiveness, and equality of access for Blacks. In D. Slaughter & D. Johnson (Eds.), *Visible now: Blacks in private schools* (pp. 143–156). Westport, CT: Greenwood.

Curran, R. E. (1983). "Splendid poverty": Jesuit slaveholding in Maryland, 1805–1838. In *Catholics in the Old South: Essays in church and culture* (pp. 125–146). Macon, GA: Mercer University Press.

Davis, C. (1990). *The History of Black Catholics in the United States.* New York: Crossroad Press.

Drake, S. C., & Cayton, H. (1945). *Black metropolis: A study of Negro life in a northern city.* New York: Harper & Row.

Franklin, V. P. (1979). *The education of Black Philadelphia: The social and educational history of a minority community, 1900–1950.* Philadelphia: University of Pennsylvania Press.

Franklin, V. P. (1981). Continuity and discontinuity in Black and immigrant minority education: A historical assessment. In D. Ravitch & R. Goodenow (Eds.), *Educating an urban people: The New York City experience* (pp. 44–66). New York: Teachers College Press.

Franklin, V. P. (1983). Ethos and education: The impact of educational activities on minority ethnic identity in the United States. *Review of Research in Education, 10,* 3–23.

Franklin, V. P. (1992). *Black self-determination: A cultural history of African American resistance.* Brooklyn, NY: Lawrence Hill Books.

Franklin, V. P., & McDonald, E. B. (1988). Blacks in urban Catholic schools in the United States: A historical perspective. In D. Slaughter and D. Johnson (Eds.), *Visible now: Blacks in private schools* (pp. 93–108). Westport, CT: Greenwood.

Gerdes, Sister M. R. (1988, Spring-Summer). To educate and evangelize: Black Catholic schools of the Oblate Sisters, 1821–1880. *U.S. Catholic Historian, 7,* 183–199.

Greeley, A. (1980). *Catholic high schools and minority students.* New Brunswick, NJ: Transaction Books.

LaFarge, J. (1954). *The manner is ordinary.* New York: Harcourt Brace.

Keith, T. Z. (1982). *Academic achievement of minority students enrolled in Catholic and public high schools.* Unpublished doctoral dissertation, Duke University, Durham, NC.

Keith, T. Z., & Page, E. B. (1985). Do Catholic high schools improve minority student achievement? *American Educational Research Journal, 22,* 337–349.

McDonogh, G. W. (1993). *Black and Catholic in Savannah, Georgia.* Knoxville: University of Tennessee Press.

McNally, M. (1987). A peculiar institution: A history of Catholic parish life in the Southeast, 1850–1980. In J. Dolan (Ed.), *The American Catholic parish: A history from 1850 to the present* (Vol. I; pp. 117–234). New York: Paulist Press.

Miller, R. M. (1983). Failed mission: The Catholic Church and Black Catholics in the Old South. In R. Miller & J. Wakelyn (Eds.), *Catholics in the Old South* (pp. 149–170). Macon, GA: Mercer University Press.

Misch, E. J. (1974). The Catholic Church and the Negro, 1865–1884. *Integrated Education, 12*, 36–40.

National Office of Black Catholics (NOBC). (1976). The crisis in Catholic education in the Black community. *Integrated Education, 14*, 14–17.

Nickels, M. W. (1988). *Black Catholic protest and the Federated Colored Catholics, 1917–1933*. New York: Garland.

Ochs, S. J. (1990). *Desegregating the altar: The Josephites and the struggle for Black priests, 1871–1960*. Baton Rouge: Louisiana State University Press.

Phelps, Sister J. T. (1988, Spring-Summer). John R. Slattery's missionary strategies. *U.S. Catholic Historian, 7*, 201–214.

Portier, W. (1986). John R. Slattery's vision for the evangelization of American Blacks. *U.S. Catholic Historian, 5*, 19–44.

Rector, T. A. (1982). Black nuns as educators. *The Journal of Negro Education, 51*, 238–253.

Richardson, J. M. (1986). *Christian Reconstruction: The American Missionary Association and southern Blacks, 1861–1890*. Athens: University of Georgia Press.

Sanders, J. W. (1977). *The education of an urban minority: Catholics in Chicago, 1833–1965*. New York: Oxford University Press.

Schillo, G. (1980, April). *Non-Catholics in Catholic schools: A challenge to evangelization*. Paper presented at the annual meeting of the National Catholic Educational Association, New Orleans.

Slaughter, D. T., & Schneider, B. L. (1986). *Newcomers: Blacks in private schools*. Washington, DC: National Institute of Education.

Spalding, D. (1969, October). The Negro Catholic Congresses, 1889–1894. *The Catholic Historical Review, 55*, 337–357.

St. John, E. P. (1977). *A study of selected developing colleges and universities: Xavier University*. Washington, DC: U.S. Office of Education.

Traxler, Sister M. E. (1969, Winter). American Catholics and Negroes. *Phylon*, pp. 355–366.

Vitullo-Martin, T. (1979). *Catholic inner-city schools: The future*. Washington, DC: U.S. Catholic Conference.

CHAPTER 3

Making a Way Out of No Way: The Oblate Sisters of Providence and St. Frances Academy in Baltimore, Maryland, 1828 to the Present

Vernon C. Polite

African Americans have affiliated with Catholicism and benefited from Catholic schooling since the early colonial era. Records from the 1500s document that some of the earliest Africans and African-Caribbean settlers in the colonies professed Catholicism (Davis, 1990). The relationship between white Catholics and African Americans in the Louisiana Territory was somewhat enhanced during the eighteenth century with the period of the French Code Noir (1724–1803), which prescribed a more liberal treatment of freeborn Black and freed mixed-race residents in the French and Spanish Catholic Louisiana Territory. As a result of the Territory's laws, several African American girls were educated at the Ursuline Academy in New Orleans in 1727 (McDermott & Hunt, 1991). More than 2,000 African and mixed-race settlers, freed under the provisions of the Code Noir, migrated to Louisiana following San Domingo's slave revolt in 1791 (Williams, 1983), and thousands of others chose to migrate to Maryland. These French-speaking African and mixed-race immigrants in both Louisiana and Maryland were generally characterized as wealthy, educated, and avowed Roman Catholics.

Because of the depreciated tobacco profits in the early 1800s, African Americans moved away from the Chesapeake region of Virginia and Maryland to the cotton production states of the deep South. However, more than 100,000 African Americans remained in Maryland in the 1820s.

 ISBN 0-8077-3530-2 (cloth).

They were a mixture of freeborn, freed, and slaves, 80% of whom were Catholics (Dedeaux, 1944).

Davis (1990) reminds us that during the early decades of the nineteenth century, slavery was well ingrained in all aspects of southern life, and the Catholic Church was no exception. In fact, many Catholic religious communities of priests were slaveowners, particularly the Jesuits, Vincentians, and Sulpicians. Ownership of slaves by the Catholic laity in the South was not uncommon. This was particularly true in Maryland, Missouri, and Kentucky, where Catholics were more likely to live. It is significant, given the menacing social conditions of the time, that a community of women, particularly women of African heritage, would emerge to establish an academy for the exclusive education of African American girls and a religious community of vowed nuns.

In this chapter, I examine the founding and extraordinary achievements of the Oblate Sisters of Providence, the oldest religious community of Roman Catholic women of African descent.

THE FOUNDING OF THE OBLATE SISTERS OF PROVIDENCE AND ST. FRANCES ACADEMY, 1828–1972

The Oblates, as they are affectionately known, opened St. Frances Academy for Colored Girls in 1828 in Baltimore, 19 years before Elizabeth Cady Stanton would organize the first American women's rights convention (Sellers, 1975) and more than 30 years prior to the signing of the Emancipation Proclamation. In fact, it was not until 61 years later, in 1889, that the First Colored Catholic Congress would clearly define the purpose of Catholic schools for African American youths in its general statement to the assembly:

> The education of a people being the great and fundamental means of elevating it to the higher planes to which all Christian civilizations tend, we pledge ourselves to aid in establishing, wherever we are to be found, Catholic Schools, embracing the primary and higher branches of knowledge, as in them and through them alone can we expect to reach the large masses of colored children now growing up in this country without a semblance of Christian education (cited in *Three Catholic Afro-American Congresses*, 1893/1978, p. 68.)

The founding of such a community of African American teaching women obviously met with resistance, particularly within the Catholic Church. The Oblates' founder, Mother Mary Elizabeth Lange, and three other African American women, in alliance with their spiritual director, Father James Hector Nicholas Joubert de la Muraile, S.S., were truly "making a way out of no way" when they secured permission from the Catholic hierarchy to open St. Frances Academy and brought into existence the new religious order.

The Founding of St. Frances Academy and the Oblates

The 166-year chronicle of formal Catholic schooling for African American students commenced with the founding of St. Frances Academy for Colored Girls in Baltimore in 1828. The permission to form the religious community known as the Oblate Sisters of Providence was granted the following year (1829). The Oblates were formally recognized by Pope Gregory XVI in 1831 (Dedeaux, 1944). The two prominent co-founders, Elizabeth Lange (known later as Sister Mary and Mother Lange) and Maria Magdalen Balas (known as Sister Marie Frances), were freeborn Black refugees from the insurrection in San Domingo (the former French possession in the West Indies known today as the island of Hispaniola) who were trained teachers (Davis, 1990; Hadrick, 1964). The two co-founders were joined by Almaide Duchemin (Sister Theresa), whose parents were murdered in San Domingo, and another Caribbean refugee, Rosina Boegue (known as Sister Mary Rose). Father Joubert, a French Sulpician priest, served as their spiritual director and shared the title of founder (Dedeaux, 1944).

The French-Caribbean background of the four founding women is most significant, particularly from a racial perspective. They were of mixed and free Black ancestry, not unlike a large percentage of the refugees from San Domingo who relocated mainly in Maryland and Louisiana in the early 1800s (Dedeaux, 1944). The racially mixed offspring of whites and Blacks were divided into 128 categories: The "mulatto" was the child of a "pure" Black and a "pure" white, the child of a white and a "mulatto" was a "quadroon," and so on.

According to James (1982), prior to the slave revolution in San Domingo the social conditions were such that every "mulatto" was free, "not by law, but because White men were so few in comparison with the slaves that the masters sought to bind these racial intermediates to themselves rather than let them swell the ranks of enemies" (p. 37). The French Code Noir of 1685 legalized marriages between white masters and slaves, meaning that their offspring were freeborn. These freeborn children of mixed ancestry were educated, and many were landholders. Thus a third race emerged on San Domingo during the eighteenth century (James, 1982).

There was significant social distancing and tension among the white masters, the slave population, and the free Black and mixed-ancestry population, particularly as the last group's numbers increased during the middle and late 1700s (James, 1982). Many of the mixed-ancestry San Domingians came to reject their privileged white ancestry, supporting the slave revolution in San Domingo, while others saw themselves as freepersons of privilege because of their white ancestry (Williams, 1983)—but all came to be perceived as a powerful and dangerous force against the white masters, largely because of their worldly experiences and education. According to James (1982), the "Mulattos educated in Paris (where they experienced total freedom) . . . had come home [San Domingo] and their education and accomplishments filled the colonists with hatred and envy and fear" (p. 56). Thereafter their rights to travel to France were revoked because "[they] learnt things that were not good for them" (James, 1982; p. 56).

The "educated mulattoes" sought relief from the social pressure and discrimination that they experienced in San Domingo, from both the slaves and the masters. The social conflict erupted in civil war. In 1791 San Domingo, one of the richest Caribbean possessions of France, became embroiled in a 12-year revolution led by Toussaint L'Ouverture (James, 1982). Those free Black and mixed-ancestry San Domingians who had financial means fled to the United States, especially to Catholic Maryland, to escape the revolution. In the 1820s, Baltimore had the largest community of African American Catholics in the United States (Dedeaux, 1944). St. Frances Academy opened in 1828 with 24 students—11 boarders, 9 nonresidents, and 4 Black religious aspirants (Hadrick, 1964). The Academy was housed at several different locations during the 40-year period before the Oblates were able to build St. Frances at its present site on Chase Street in Baltimore in 1871 (Baptiste, 1939).

The Oblates were pioneers in the field of education. Although a small number of abolitionist-sponsored schools had surfaced in New England and the mid-Atlantic states for the education of African Americans (Seller, 1975), the Oblates were the first to provide a comprehensive educational agenda and curriculum for African American students. Fortunately, they met little formal resistance to providing education for African Americans in the 1830s in Maryland (Hadrick, 1964).

It was not until the late 1800s that the two quintessential African American ideologues of the nineteenth century, Booker T. Washington and W.E.B. Du Bois, would emerge. They would offer two diametrically opposed educational agendas for the race. Washington would stress the industrial education path available at Hampton and Tuskegee Institutes, while Du Bois would emphasize the importance of a classical education for the "talented tenth" of the race as reflected by the curricula available at Atlanta and Howard Universities (Lewis, 1994). The Oblates, however, created a curriculum for African American girls before the influence of Washington and Du Bois and without a model or guide. Interestingly, the curriculum model developed by the Oblates provided African American girls with both the classical education proposed by Du Bois and the vocational education proposed by Washington.

The sisters understood the economy and the job market available to African American women at that time, but they also believed in a solid academic preparation, a philosophy that has remained a part of St. Frances Academy to this day. Students during the early 1830s were trained in religion, French, arithmetic, geography, history, grammar, orthography, algebra, natural philosophy, and composition, as well as sewing, embroidering, tapestry making, tufted work, bead work, lace embroidering, wax flower making, flower and fruit arranging, elementary drawing, painting, and vocal and instrumental music (Baptiste, 1939). In every possible venue, the Oblates taught their students about the achievements and history of their race, including the history and treatment of Africans and their posterity in the Caribbean, Europe, and the United States (Baptiste, 1939). Their foresight was remarkable, especially given the fact that only 10% of the African American population could read at the time of the Civil War in 1865 (Caliver, 1933/1969).

The nuns also managed to avoid complete social isolation within the Church by maintaining ties with the Catholic hierarchy and the Catholic school system in Maryland. Although there was widespread racism within the Church, the Oblates embraced the structure of the Church, relying on Father Joubert for specific religious support (Baptiste, 1939). Father Joubert also served as a buffer against the opposition from within the Church. Being a part of the Catholic system was an extremely valuable asset during the early days, when there were no national mandates for establishing schools, particularly for African American students. In 1863, in the midst of the Civil War and national economic strife, the Oblates opened a second school for African American children and women in Philadelphia (Davis, 1990). Their influence reached beyond the sphere of education, for they were committed to assisting wherever needed. The Oblates expanded their mission beyond education in 1832 to include nursing victims of the cholera epidemic and directing St. Mary's Infirmary in Baltimore between 1832 to 1850 (Baptiste, 1939). The Oblates also operated an orphanage in New York between 1867 and 1872.

The Oblate Sisters and St. Frances from the Mid-Nineteeth Century to 1974

The community did experience isolation and limited support from the Catholic Church following Father Joubert's death in 1843. In fact, the religious hierarchy suggested that there was no need for a Black religious community and encouraged the Oblates to disband (Davis, 1990). Mother Lange and the Oblates persisted and later received spiritual support from a Redemptorist priest, Father Thaddeus Anwander, in 1847, four years after the death of Father Joubert. The Oblates were led through some of the most difficult times in the history of community and the history of African Americans by Mother Lange until her death at the age of 95 in 1882 (Rector, 1982).

During the mid-1800s, the Oblates maintained St. Frances Academy and began several other educational ventures, but it became substantially more difficult to pursue their first vocation, the education of children of African descent, because slaveholders in the South opposed schooling for Africans (Woodson, 1915). African American Catholics enjoyed equal civil rights in Pennsylvania, Delaware, Virginia, and Maryland but experienced harsh treatment in New England, New Jersey, South Carolina, and Georgia (Hadrick, 1964). The *Dred Scott* decision of 1851, the rise of the Republican party, the fugitive slave laws, the Underground Railroad, John Brown's raids in 1859, and the Civil War itself made education for African Americans an extremely risky business (Hadrick, 1964).

Following the Civil War and Reconstruction, the Oblates turned to the matter of improving the academic preparation of their members. They were rejected for many years by Catholic institutions of higher education; but in 1923 St. Scholastica College in Atchison, Kansas, run by the Benedictine Sisters, became the first Catholic college to admit the Oblate Sisters to their summer classes. St. Scholastica was followed by Villanova College (in Pennsylvania) in 1925 and St. Louis University in 1927. In 1933 The Catholic University of America admitted three Oblates, the first persons of color to study there (Hadrick, 1964). Although the sisters pursued education in the best Catholic universities, they believed they could do the most good by teaching and administering grade and high schools rather than colleges (Baptiste, 1939).

The Oblates' influence was felt throughout the African American community. Over the years, thousands of African American women were educated by the Oblate Sisters. The subjects offered were English, Latin, modern languages, social studies, mathematics, science, physical education, home economics, religion, and vocal and instrumental music. Many of their graduates became public school teachers, particularly in the District of Columbia (Baptiste, 1939).

As of the mid-1990s, there are 145 Oblates; however, their actual annual membership has varied widely over the years. One report from the mid-nineteenth century indicated that there were as few as 22 Oblates, while another reported as many as 350 in the 1950s (Rector, 1982). In spite of their small numbers, their impact on African Americans in the United

States has been significant. In addition to St. Frances Academy, which is owned and operated by the Oblates, the nuns have directed schools and missions in Florida, Illinois, Maryland, Michigan, Missouri, New Jersey, New York, Pennsylvania, South Carolina, the District of Columbia, and Costa Rica.

St. Frances Academy has survived for more than a century and a half under the direction of the Oblate Sisters of Providence. The school closed for repairs and reorganization in 1972–74. The following section details the effectiveness of St. Frances Academy for urban African American youth from 1974 to the present.

ST. FRANCES ACADEMY FROM 1974 TO THE PRESENT

When the Oblates reopened St. Frances in the fall of 1974, the 146-year-old school, with an enrollment of less than 150 high school students, had undergone significant renovations. There were upgrades of the school's physical plant that included science and computer laboratories and improved heating and cooling facilities. The building itself dates from 1870; consequently many other structural upgrades were needed, but the facilities are in "good" condition. One major change, however, was not structural; rather it was the nuns' philosophy of schooling for African American youth. The school became a coeducational institution, accepting its first African American male students in the fall of 1974. Given the deleterious educational and social outcomes for African American males in public schools and society (see Garibaldi, 1992; Polite, 1993a, 1993b), the Oblates resolved to begin to educate this population. Large numbers of African American males did not immediately enroll in the school, presumably due to the long and celebrated history of the school as an all-girl academy. In fact, Sister John Francis, the current principal at St. Frances, recalled that as late as 1985 the ratio of boys to girls was one to five. However, the numbers of boys and girls enrolled during the 1994–95 school year were nearly equal, with slightly more boys than girls.

Additionally, the overall demographics of the school have changed drastically. The history of St. Frances Academy reflects the institution's mission to serve a privileged class of African American girls. However, the students who now attend St. Frances are representative of Baltimore's working class and unemployed. Nearly 99% of the students reside within the city of Baltimore. In this respect, St. Frances is not unlike other inner-city Catholic schools. The records from the academic year 1990–91 indicate that 30% of St. Frances students lived in households described as below the poverty line and 62% lived in single-parent households. These data were extracted from statistics compiled by Sister John Francis, O.S.P., from 1986 through 1991. Amazingly, 85% of these graduates became the first generation in their families to attend college. Students commonly enter St. Frances with inadequate academic preparation. A small number have been identified as learning-disabled, and others have come from adverse social experiences in urban and suburban public schools. To address the academic deficits of the majority of the incoming students, a summer institute is held to reteach and remediate.

The typical St. Frances Academy student does not fit the usual white Catholic school student profile. Given the school's location in what is now one of the poorest communities in Baltimore, the students are representative of that environment. Their parents, guardians, and extended families have, in most cases, made extreme sacrifices of time, energy, and money to provide a Catholic education for their children. For many of these parents, St. Frances is the last hope for improved educational opportunities for their children (Polite, 1992). In this respect, the new St. Frances is not unlike urban Catholic schools that most closely resemble the ideal of the common school model; that is, they educate children from different backgrounds and achieve promising academic outcomes. Research refutes the notion commonly held by the general public that inner-city Catholic schools educate a privileged group of African American students. Rather, these students come predominantly from the African American working class; 72% come from families with household incomes of less than $15,000 annually (Polite, 1992).

The academic outcomes at St. Frances are indeed remarkable. As many as 95% of the school's graduates attend postsecondary schools, and the records from follow-up studies of the graduates reveal that more than 80% of the graduates who attend college actually graduate. Fewer than 5% of the students drop out of St. Frances. This positive student attitude toward postsecondary schooling is typical of African American Catholic school students.

A study conducted in 1986 found that 82% of urban African American Catholic high school students believed that they would complete college, compared to 74% of white students in the study sample (Benson, Yeager, Wood, Guerra, & Manno, 1986). Empirical data show a convincing correlation between urban Catholic school attendance and various indices of educational attainment. The correlation is particularly significant for the large percentage of African American students currently enrolled in urban Catholic schools.

Regarding governance, St. Frances is owned and controlled by the Oblate Sisters of Providence with permission of the local diocese and bishop. The Oblates' congregation is governed by a five-member, elected council. The Council is responsible for appointing the principal of the school, overseeing the curriculum and major functions, providing teachers from the community and other personnel, and awarding substantial financial assistance to students. Sister John Francis, the principal at St. Frances Academy, reports twice a year to the Council on a multiplicity of issues related to the school, particularly its financial status. An independent auditor is responsible for overseeing the finances of the Oblates and the school. At the present time, few urban Catholic schools are controlled by religious communities like the Oblates. Most receive direction, supervision, and evaluation from the bishop through the diocesan office (Drahmann, 1985).

Tuition at urban Catholic schools is typically kept reasonable through careful financial management. The annual tuition cost at St. Frances was $3,200 for the 1993–94 school year. Nationally, the average parochial school tuition cost was $2,299 at the secondary level during the 1989–90 school year (Kealey, 1990). By comparison, public schools spent an average of $4,000 per student, and some private nonparochial schools charge as much as $9,000 annually per student.

Fundraising, one of the principal responsibilities of Catholic school parents, has helped to ensure the relatively low tuition at St. Frances. More importantly, fundraising at St. Frances involves each family in the activities of the school, leaving few opportunities for social distancing between the school and home. The school sponsors an annual May festival as its principal fundraiser. The Oblate Sisters of Providence, through their motherhouse, provide supplemental financial assistance to the school.

St. Frances parents understand the culture of the school, and the faculty understands the culture of the students' home. Parental support is a key factor in the effectiveness of urban Catholic schools; this is particularly true at St. Frances Academy.

St. Frances, like other Catholic schools, customarily and consistently expects and rewards academic diligence, personal development, and student demonstrations of traditional Christian values. Unlike the faculties of contemporary Catholic schools, which are composed mostly of lay teachers, the St. Frances faculty is composed of eight nuns of the Oblates community, one nun who is a member of the Sisters of Notre Dame, three Christian Brothers, and five lay teachers; all teachers except the Christian Brothers are African Americans. Two of the lay teachers are recent graduates of the Academy. In observing the teachers in their workplace, I got a strong sense of commitment and extremely high expectations of the students. Catholic school teachers, students, and parents alike generally report that academic excellence is highly valued, and administrators indicate that the morale is high among their teachers (Yeager et al., 1985). Because they encourage their students to struggle against negative peer pressure and other social ills, St. Frances and other urban Catholic schools are viewed by their faculties and parents as positive learning centers where students' academic, spiritual, and social needs are met.

Studies have also found that African American students attending Catholic schools score better on achievement tests than do their counterparts in public schools (Greeley, 1982). This difference is likely due in part to the strong emphasis placed on required basic courses in Catholic schools, a correlate identified with effective schools. Nearly 50% more African Americans in Catholic schools completed courses in geometry, and 47% more completed courses in algebra II than did the national average. Lee and Stewart (1989) found that 60% of African American Catholic school students took chemistry, compared to 32% of African American students nationwide; 87% completed courses in general science, compared to 79% of African Americans nationwide; and 100% completed a biology course, compared to 89% of African Americans nationwide. Additionally, Catholic school students generally are more likely to be enrolled in a college preparatory program and to complete more mathematics courses than are their public school counterparts (Lee & Bryk, 1989).

Marks and Lee's (1989) work indicates that African Americans who attended Catholic schools score significantly higher in the area of reading than do their counterparts in public schools but score significantly lower than their white counterparts in Catholic and public schools. Lee and Stewart (1989) report that while African American students in Catholic schools score consistently above their counterparts in public schools in both mathematics and science, they score below white Catholic school students. This remains an area of concern for Catholic educators.

Although the college entrance tests scores for students at St. Frances are low when compared with national statistics, the principal, Sister John Francis, is quite pleased, given the academic deficits common among these students upon arriving at the school. What is impressive, given the size of the school, is its curriculum. Not unlike the typical urban Catholic school, St. Frances provides a curriculum that focuses on college awareness and prepares students to be successful in postsecondary education. All students are required to take four years of college preparatory English, mathematics (for example, algebra I & II, geometry, trigonometry, precalculus, and honors mathematics), and the sciences; three years of a foreign language (Spanish or French); four years of history; keyboarding and word processing. Knowledge of the accomplishment of African Americans is taught in African American studies and is incorporated into all classes.

The curriculum also addresses the affective development of the African American students. All students are required to engage in community outreach service during their third and fourth years at the school, providing 60 hours of service per year to a community agency. In the past the students have worked with sexually abused children, with senior citizens, and in nursing homes. Upon completion of their community service, the students are required to write a paper that guides the student through a structured reflective exercise. Given the troubled environments in which many of the students live, the school has established a Boys-to-Men program, which provides mentoring and business experiences, a Rights of Passage program, and peer tutoring for both boys and girls.

Although St. Frances does not have a gymnasium, both the girls' and boys' basketball teams were among the top 20 in the region in 1993. In addition to basketball, the school offers track and cross-country. Nearly every student participates in some extracurricular sport or other activity.

The school climate at St. Frances is also typical of most inner-city Catholic schools and consistent with the effective schools paradigm (Edmonds, 1979). With its small teacher to student ratio of 1 to 20, teachers experience a strong sense of work efficacy. Catholic schools, including St. Frances, generally are able to create a climate characterized by caring discipline, order, and a strong sense of community. With fewer than 150 students and 100% African American enrollment, St. Frances clearly has an advantage over its neighboring public schools, some of which have as many as 2,500 students enrolled. Most (93%) of the Catholic high schools examined in the study by Yeager and colleagues (1985) prohibit students from leaving the school grounds during the day, and this is also true at St. Frances. Additionally, the dress code seems to minimize peer competition. As in other urban Catholic high schools, the St. Frances staff on the average expel only 1% of their students, suspend fewer than 3%, and experience few behavior problems (Yeager et al., 1985).

When questioned about evangelization and the number of students who are actually Catholic, Sister John Francis indicated that there was no overt push to compel the students to convert to Catholicism at St. Frances, mentioning that many of the students had developed rather strong religious convictions prior to enrolling at the Academy. All students are required to take and pass courses in Catholic theology and teachings. Religious services, which are often student-led, are held in the school's chapel each month. Interestingly, only 25% of students identified themselves as Catholic; the overwhelming majority are Protestant. It is important to note that while many African American parents choose Catholic schools for their children as an alternative to the problem-plagued public schools, Catholic schools like St. Frances do not exist solely as a refuge for students who would otherwise attend nonproductive public schools. Catholic schools are not designed to serve merely as private institutions that accept all academically motivated students who can pay the tuition; they are also parochial schools that have as one of their missions the teaching of Christianity within the context of the Catholic tradition. A general understanding apparently exists among the Catholic religious hierarchy that Catholic schools, such as St. Frances, must remain an option for the teaching of Christian values and morals to those who desire and need them most. A special preference must be afforded the disadvantaged and unchurched urban youths. This assertion is not categorically accepted by all Catholics (Lyke, 1991).

CONCLUSION

A survey of 113,000 adults conducted in 1990 concluded that African Americans who attended Catholic schools were more likely than most Americans to complete high school and college (Lachman & Kosmin, 1991). Only 18% of the African Americans who attended Catholic schools dropped out of high school, compared with 31% of the total African American population and 21% of the general population. The graduates of St. Frances Academy in Baltimore are evidence that urban youth can achieve academic success.

The opportunities for the nation's inner-city children to acquire a quality education seemingly become less likely with each passing academic year. From all indications, the problems of public education are not only multifarious but also more negatively impact African Americans and other disadvantaged minority students. A Catholic school, such as St. Frances Academy, in a blight-stricken community is more than a mere bright spot; it prepares its students by providing the intellectual, economic, and spiritual tools needed to attack social injustices. While public schools are crying out for quality education, social action programs, local school-based management, community building among staff and students, parental involvement, and volunteer support, these aspects are typical operating realities in the urban Catholic schools that serve largely African American students.

The Oblate Sisters of Providence take their rightful place among the great contributors to the betterment of the African American community. The religious community, with its history of more than a century and a half, is one of the oldest African American organizations in the country with an unbroken history. The Oblates made a way out of no way!

A NOTE ON THE DATA

The data reported in this chapter were culled from in-depth interviews with Sister Mary Reparata Clarke, O.S.P., a teacher at the Academy and a member of the Oblates for 50 years, and Sister John Francis Schilling, O.S.P., an Oblate for 25 years, a counselor at the school for 9 years, and the current principal of St. Frances; observations at St. Frances Academy; and document analyses conducted at St. Frances Academy on Chase Street in Baltimore and the Oblates Sisters' Alumni Office and Archives, housed at Our Lady of Mount Providence Convent in Baltimore. The interviews and field notes were analyzed in accordance with the coding, sorting, and verification strategies recommended in Bogdan and Biklen (1992).

REFERENCES

Baptiste, M. (1939). *A study of the foundation and educational objectives of the Congregation of the Oblate Sisters of Providence and of the achievement of these objectives as seen in their schools.* Unpublished master's thesis, Villanova College, Villanova, PA.

Benson, P. L., Yeager, R. J., Wood, P. K., Guerra, M. J., & Manno, B. V. (1986). *Catholic high schools: Their impact on low-income students.* Washington, DC: National Catholic Educational Association.

Bogdan, R., & Biklen, S. (1992). *Qualitative research in education.* Boston: Allyn & Bacon.

Caliver, A. (1969). *Secondary education for Negroes* (U.S. Office of Education Bulletin No. 17 [1932]; National Survey of Secondary Education Monograph No. 7). New York: Negro Universities Press. (Original work published 1933)

Davis, C. (1990). *The history of Black Catholics in the United States.* New York: Crossroad.

Dedeaux, M. L. (1944). *The influence of St. Frances Academy on Negro Catholic education in the nineteenth century.* Unpublished master's thesis, Villanova College, Villanova, PA.

Drahmann, T. (1985). *Governance and administration in the Catholic school.* Washington, DC: National Catholic Educational Association.

Edmonds, R. (1979). Effective schools for urban poor. *Educational Leadership, 37*(1), 15–18, 20–24.

Garibaldi, A. M. (1992). Educating and motivating African American males to succeed. *Journal of Negro Education, 61*(1), 4–11.

Greeley, A. W. (1982). *Catholic high schools and minority students.* New Brunswick, NJ: Transaction Books.

Hadrick, E. M. (1964). *Contributions of the Oblate Sisters of Providence to Catholic edu-*

cation in the United States and Cuba 1829–1962. Unpublished master's thesis, The Catholic University of America, Washington, DC.

James, C. L. R. (1982). *The Black Jacobins: Toussaint L'Ouverture and San Domingo revolution.* London: Allsion & Busby.

Kealey, R. J. (1990). *The United States Catholic schools and their finances, 1989.* Washington, DC: National Catholic Educational Association.

Lachman, S., & Kosmin, B. A. (1991). First national survey of religious identifications of Americans conducted by CUNY Graduate Center researchers. Unpublished raw data.

Lee, V. E., & Bryk, A. S. (1989). A multilevel model of the social distribution of high school achievement. *Sociology of Education, 62,* 172–192.

Lee, V. E., & Stewart, C. (1989). *National Assessment of Educational Progress, proficiency in mathematics and science, 1985–1986: Catholic and public schools compared.* Washington, DC: National Catholic Educational Association.

Lewis, D. L. (1994). *W. E. B. Du Bois: Biography of a race 1868–1919.* New York: Holt.

Lyke, J. P. (1991, November). *Catholic schools: The lifeblood of evangelization.* Paper presented at the special meeting of the National Congress on Catholic Schools, Washington, DC.

Marks, H. M., & Lee, V. E. (1989). *National Assessment of Educational Progress, proficiency in reading, 1985–1986: Catholic and public schools compared.* Washington, DC: National Catholic Educational Association.

McDermott, M. L., & Hunt, T. C. (1991). Catholic schools: A first in Louisiana. *Momentum, 22*(4), 46–50.

Polite, V. C. (1992). Getting the job done well: African American students and Catholic schools. *Journal of Negro Education, 61*(2), 211–222.

Polite, V. C. (1993a). If only we knew then what we know now: Foiled opportunities to learn in suburbia. *Journal of Negro Education, 63*(3), 337–354.

Polite, V. C. (1993b). Educating African American males in suburbia: Quality education? . . . Caring environment? *Journal of African American Male Studies, 2*(1), 1–25.

Rector, T. A. (1982). Black nuns as educators. *Journal of Negro Education, 51*(3), 238–253.

Sellers, C. G. (1975). *As it happened: A history of the United States.* New York: McGraw Hill.

Three Catholic Afro-American congresses (Proceedings of the First Colored Catholic Congress). (1978). New York: Arno Press. (Original work published 1893)

Williams, E. (1983). *From Columbus to Castro: The history of the Caribbean, 1492–1969.* London: Andre Deutsche.

Woodson, C. G. (1915). *The education of the Negro prior to 1861.* New York: G. P. Putnam's Sons.

Yeager, R. J., Benson, P. L., Guerra, M. J., & Manno, B. V. (1985). *The Catholic high school: A national portrait.* Washington, DC: National Catholic Educational Association.

CHAPTER 4

Holy Angels: Pocket of Excellence

Portia H. Shields

Holy Angels School in Chicago is the largest all-Black Roman Catholic school in the nation, with 1,300 students, from preschoolers and kindergartners to high school-aged students. Upon initial examination, Holy Angels appears to be a throwback to the 1940s and early 1950s, when schools for Blacks embraced the children of working-class, upwardly mobile families whose educational values mirrored those of the teachers. The children at Holy Angels demonstrate respect for adults and schoolmates. Neither swearing nor fighting is allowed, and responses to adults of "yes" and "no" are accompanied by "ma'am" or "sir." The Reeboks, miniskirts, affected walks, and hip talk of the street are left behind for the duration of the school day. School rules are rigorously adhered to, and the students—alert, proud, responsive, and happy to be part of the Holy Angels family—strive to complete their assignments first, fastest, and best.

Approximately a hundred years old and fully accredited by the state of Illinois, Holy Angels was founded by Irish immigrants just before the turn of the century. The South Side neighborhood and parish surrounding the school grew to such affluence in the late 1920s that the church had a bishop as its leader. With the Great Depression came massive Black migration from the South and white flight from the inner city. By the end of World War II, the transition from white to Black in the Holy Angels neighborhood was complete.

The neighborhood has declined steadily since then. In its present depressed condition, it contains the greatest number of Chicago families in federally supported dwellings. The main sustenance of most of these families, two-thirds of which are headed by single parents, is welfare. The incidence of crime in this community is the highest in the city, largely due to drugs and gangs.

The astoundingly successful Holy Angels program, which runs contrary to most contemporary educational philosophy, raises some fundamental questions:

1. How does the school doctrine incorporate countermeasures into its educational setting whereby poor Black families and their children are not overwhelmed by the effects of joblessness, homelessness, and substance abuse?
2. How do Holy Angels students achieve superior academic results despite a national report that cited functional illiteracy rates as high as 40% among minority children from similar neighborhoods (National Commission on Excellence in Education, 1983) and despite the fact that many of the parents of these children can be included among the nation's approximately 23 million functionally illiterate adults?
3. How do Holy Angels faculty maximize the academic and social abilities of children categorized as disadvantaged, at risk, and unlikely to acquire the tools necessary for full participation in American society?

Since Catholic schools enroll the majority of private school populations in the country, one response would be to focus on Holy Angels private school status. Coleman (1981) compared public and Catholic schools and concluded that Catholic schools excelled in quality. There are, however, important differences in family affluence and in the school selection processes between the Catholic schools documented in Coleman's report and those at Holy Angels that cannot be reconciled. A closer examination of Holy Angels reveals that it is neither a typical Catholic school nor a typical Black Catholic school. Two distinct groups of families enroll their children in Holy Angels. The largest group, whose children comprise approximately two-thirds of the student body, lives in the surrounding neighborhood and subsists on fixed incomes; these families are headed predominantly by single mothers in their mid-30s to early 40s. The other group includes the children of younger white-collar workers, some themselves products of Holy Angels, who live in more affluent sections of Chicago and its contiguous suburbs. Seventy-five percent of the children accepted at the school are not Catholic, although the majority embrace Catholicism by the time they graduate. Children seeking admittance to Holy Angels are tested with a combination of standardized and informal tests, yet there is no cutoff score and selection is not predicated upon test results alone.

Thus, if the linchpin of success in the Catholic–private school variable is not the socioeconomic status of the students or their parents, then the leadership of the school must be the determining factor. In this context, it would be impossible to discount the influence of the Reverend George Clements, the progressive church leader who is nationally known for founding the successful "One Church—One Child" adoption program and who has himself adopted three sons (Norment, 1986). Tireless and determined, this effective leader has played a critical role at Holy Angels. When asked about what is most significant about the program at Holy Angels, Father Clements responded:

> We have faith in [our] system because it works. The products attest to this. [Our] children are at the national norms in all academic areas. In most, they are one to two levels above their public school peers and they measure up against children in more typical Catholic schools. Eighty percent of the students go on to graduate from college. (personal communication to the author, November 1, 1985)

This record of achievement, in Clements's view, motivates both parents and students to become totally involved in the Holy Angels tradition. Furthermore, he added, there are about a thousand students on the school's waiting list, despite his belief that students at Holy Angels are put under more pressure to achieve than those at most other schools.

Clements also believes that for many Holy Angels parents the very act of paying tuition contributes to greater family participation as well as increased feelings of self-worth in the children. His premise is that "what one pays for, one values more." No family is exempt from payment, there are no scholarships offered, and no federal funding is used to pay tuition for any Holy Angels student. Since Holy Angels is determined to remain financially attainable to families in its neighboring community, tuition is kept low (currently about $300 annually), and all families are required to participate in fundraising activities to subsidize the school's inexpensive tuition rate.

Strong disciplinary standards characteristic of church-related schools also contribute to the greater academic achievement of Holy Angels students. Truancy and dropout problems are virtually nonexistent. Sanctions are applied in a consistent, uniform, and incremental fashion, and they are expeditiously enforced. For example, an incident of tardiness incurs a 25¢ fine, but a repeat offense could mean detention. Acts of vandalism and fighting lead quickly and directly to suspension. Corporal punishment is an option if other measures fail. All children must wear the required uniforms; nail polish, jewelry, and cosmetics are not permitted. Parents who find the regulations too restrictive are advised to seek schooling for their children elsewhere.

THE ROLE OF FAMILIES

Holy Angels accepts families rather than individuals. The philosophy of the school is that families need to become their own agents for change, and Holy Angels places the family in this pivotal role in its students' education. The family's role permeates the schooling process; parental cooperation and responsibility are key requirements that factor into the Holy Angels success equation. School programs and activities have evolved around a systematic attempt to unite families by taking a holistic approach to their intellectual, moral, and spiritual development.

Continuous, sustained family cooperation and interest are mandatory. Parents must pick up their children's report cards in person, and they must confer regularly with teachers concerning progress or problems as well as attend monthly school meetings. No excuses or exceptions are tolerated; failure to cooperate with these mandates results in suspension.

Ultimately, the parents of Holy Angels students are held responsible for their children's successful completion of daily homework assignments. Parents are required to sign and return forms verifying that they have seen their children's homework. To that end, teachers are trained to make certain that students understand their home assignments, since many of the undereducated parents are often unable to interpret homework or to assist their children with it.

Parents are also required to provide a home environment that is conducive to their children's study. During the week, parents must prohibit their children from playing outside or watching television, not for the sake of punishment but to promote the children's concentration on their studies and to eliminate distractions. Parents must also take their children to church services every Sunday.

If this high level of parental involvement at Holy Angels seems burdensome, it is offset by the frequent rewarding of parents' efforts. Each year on Father's Day, a special ceremony singles out fathers to receive certificates, medals, and accolades from their children. (Students without fathers or those who have no male family member available are assigned surrogate fathers.) To further underscore the significance of family input to student learning and other achievement at Holy Angels, parents are called up to the stage with their children during graduation ceremonies and they receive their children's diplomas.

THE ROLE OF THE FACULTY

Father Clements attributes the success of the school and its prominence to Father Paul Smith, who, for 25 years, has served as principal at Holy Angels. Father Smith has the primary responsibility for hiring and supervising teachers. He has traveled as far away as Canada to recruit the caliber of determined, well-educated, highly motivated, and caring teachers who can make a difference in the lives of Holy Angels students. Teachers of the "missionary" persuasion, who would excuse children and tolerate lower standards of performance out of pity for the children's circumstances, are not retained at Holy Angels for very long. The faculty includes nuns (some recruited out of retirement), lay teachers (several of whom are themselves graduates of Holy Angels), and instructors from a local volunteer teacher program.

Once hired, teachers are trained in the Holy Angels excellence doctrine, which espouses the belief that Holy Angels students can learn regardless of their personal or family circumstances or the pathology of their environment. Teachers are trained to manifest this theory by using tactics that challenge students to perform at mastery levels. The goals of teacher instruction, as summarized from Holy Angels School's Statement of Philosophy, are to

1. Provide an educational program that will enable students to develop to their fullest potential
2. Provide an atmosphere of learning in which students may develop self-acceptance, belief in their own competence, and trust and confidence in their capabilities
3. Develop students' abilities to make choices and to accept the responsibilities and consequences of those choices
4. Help students master academic tasks and become competent in their studies
5. Help students learn to be purposeful and seek out the resources and responsibilities of this world in order to be eternally happy in the world to come
6. Prod the wills and imaginations of students so that they will want to become involved citizens who can respond to challenges with the courage to do what they must in order to survive and overcome obstacles

7. Provide students with an environment of discipline, structure, and order that fosters the development of self-control
8. Establish a hunger for independence and self-determination in students via an emphasis on their sense of personal worth
9. Elicit a spirit of peace that enables students to get along with their peers and show respect and tolerance for the rights and worth of others (Holy Angels School, undated, p. 1)

Teachers use entrance test results to identify children's strengths and needs and to group them accordingly. Despite a pupil–teacher ratio of approximately 37 to 1, which is certainly more than is traditionally recommended, this homogeneous arrangement is, according to the staff, a motivating force for academic improvement. Placement procedures and decisions are carefully explained to both the children and their parents.

With enthusiasm, caring, and patience, Holy Angels teachers provide the conditions necessary to stimulate their students to reach the limit of their potential. Faculty teach in self-contained classroom arrangements, demonstrating skills, carefully explaining concepts, conducting participatory (hands-on) and culturally relevant practice activities, and reviewing subject matter often. They actively engage their students in basic skills instruction that emphasizes reading, writing, and mathematics. English, history, science, and mathematics are taught in all grade levels. As would be expected, religious training, incorporating the Baltimore Catechism with traditional prayers, mass, and sacraments, is mandatory during one period of each school day.

THE ROLE OF STUDENTS

Students attend classes at Holy Angels for nearly twelve months of the year rather than the customary nine (they get a short vacation in August). The regular school day is from 8:30 A.M. to 3:00 P.M.; however, children are allowed to arrive as early as 6:00 A.M. and may remain as late as 7:00 P.M. to accommodate the schedules of working parents. Students who need additional reinforcement receive remedial instruction after school. Saturday school is mandatory for students who require even more help or for those who are inattentive during regular class time. (The very real possibility of having to spend Saturdays at school is also believed to be another of the factors that motivates Holy Angels students to concentrate and behave during the week.)

The practice of peer tutoring, or pairing students off into twos to reinforce certain skills, is also used at Holy Angels. This not only strengthens subject-matter acquisition but also encourages the development of nurturing relationships between students and fosters self-confidence and the desire to improve.

Another activity that Holy Angels students are required to engage in is called "Roots and Leaves." Through it, students volunteer to assist elderly patients in convalescent homes, reading to them, running errands, and undertaking small, but necessary, helpful tasks. For some students, this experience offers them their first opportunity to interact with a "grandparent" figure.

Student excellence is rewarded at Holy Angels, thus creating an atmosphere of healthy competition. To participate in sports, regardless of athletic prowess, students must maintain academic eligibility, yet Holy Angels has won the Catholic Youth Basketball Conference championships for the past three years. Honor rolls and awards recognize the achievements of older students, and younger students' outstanding papers are adorned with stars. Morning announcements on the school's public address system also highlight student successes.

CONCLUSION

The extent of hopelessness and despair in blighted urban areas such as those in which most of Holy Angels students reside cannot be determined; however, unemployment, social dislocation, and the erosion of traditional family values and authority relations have surely exacted their toll:

- Between 40 and 60% of students in neighborhoods such as these drop out of high school prior to graduation.
- Almost 70% of inner-city minority youth are unemployed, and most of these youngsters have little regard for the kinds of jobs that are readily available.
- A 12-year-old Black boy in the inner city has a 90% chance of becoming the victim of a violent crime in his lifetime.
- Homicide is the leading cause of death among young Black men, especially in the inner city.
- Poor Blacks in urban ghettos are robbed four times more often than other populations; their homes have a 90% chance of being burglarized (Magnet, 1987).

Recently, the National Conference on Educating Black Children (1987) met and developed a publication, *Blueprint for Action II,* which outlines ways for helping students, parents, teachers, administrators, communities, and policy makers achieve educational equity and excellence in schools that teach Black students. This effort was preceded by those of other Black educators, such as Gordon (1968), Comer (1980), and Edmonds (1986), who also prescribed remedies for successful achievement for Black families, students, and schools. Unfortunately, the strategies advocated in these scholarly pursuits have been difficult to implement or enforce in public school systems due to legal restrictions and public policies that inhibit easy implementation.

Holy Angels is not so constrained. How does Holy Angels prevent the social, psychological, and economic realities of the contiguous urban ghetto from penetrating the educational setting? The answer is simple. Holy Angels makes no attempt to ignore pressing social problems. Teachers routinely discuss the real issues that have a negative impact on the quality of their students' and their students' families' lives. Classroom discussions of these issues and events related to them assist the students in identifying alternative directions and behaviors. For example, in addition to human sexuality classes that are conducted jointly with students and parents, boys are counseled about the negative consequences of teenage pregnancy and about the male's role in and responsibility for it.

Holy Angels offers alternatives to the negative influences in innercity communities. It promises more than the tenuous survival offered to the children of the urban ghetto, and it provides more than the material rewards of literacy, academic skill, and training. It also gives these youngsters concrete evidence that they can be successful.

For these critical reasons, total family involvement and commitment are non-negotiable at Holy Angels, and the school's leadership makes absolutely no excuses for its strict policies. Holy Angels demands excellence, expects excellence, and achieves optimum effort from its faculty, parents, and students. It is this thoroughly engaged partnership that makes the difference. Observers may not agree with many of the arguably Draconian policies and practices that distinguish the Holy Angels program from other educational institutions, but they must acknowledge the program's success. In other words, one might debate the process, but the results are incontrovertibly appropriate.

The lesson to be learned from the Holy Angels experience is that in a depressed urban setting where strong family relationships are perceived to be fragile, a viable, relevant alternative to traditional educational philosophy is compulsory. By pairing energetic, committed, and involved educators with concerned and motivated parents, Holy Angels helps its students achieve their maximum potential irrespective of their economic status or social standing. Holy Angels provides the actual environment for Black urban poor students to accomplish their goals in spite of the social, health, and economic obstacles that disproportionately affect them and their families. As a result of Holy Angels success, educators may be required to rethink their prescriptive methodologies for educating the children of the urban poor.

REFERENCES

Coleman, J. (1981). Quality and equality in American education: Public and Catholic schools. *Phi Delta Kappan, 63,* 159–164.

Comer, J. (1980). *School power: Implications of an intervention project.* New York: Free Press.

Edmonds, R. R. (1986). Characteristics of effective schools. In U. Neisser (Ed.), *The school achievement of minority children* (pp. 93–104). Hillsdale, NJ: Erlbaum.

Gordon, I. (1968). *Parent involvement in compensatory education.* Urbana: University of Illinois Press.

Holy Angels School. (undated). *Statement of Philosophy.*

Magnet, M. (1987, May). America's underclass: What to do? *Fortune,* pp. 130–150.

National Commission on Excellence in Education. (1983). *A nation at risk: The imperative for educational reform.* Washington, DC: U.S. Government Printing Office.

National Conference on Educating Black Children. (1987). *A blueprint for action II.* Washington, DC: Author.

Norment, L. (1986, March). One Church—One Child. *Ebony,* pp. 68–75.

PART II

Personal Memories and Reflections

CHAPTER 5

Segregation and Academic Excellence: African American Catholic Schools in the South

Jacqueline Jordan Irvine

Writing an educational memoir is an intimidating and humbling assignment. Reflections necessarily force an individual to grapple with events of the past that have been conveniently forgotten, misinterpreted, or exaggerated in the tumultuous passage from childhood to adulthood. However, writing this chapter turned out to be both a pleasant and revealing experience, and I am pleased to share these thoughts with readers.

My story is based in Phenix City, Alabama, from 1952 through 1964. Phenix City is an eastern Alabama town that borders Columbus, Georgia, the third largest city in that state, and Fort Benning, Georgia, a large military installation. In retrospect, Phenix City during the 1950s and 1960s was like so many small southern towns that African American people like to forget—segregated, oppressive, poor, cruel, abusive, and dehumanizing. The quality of the all-Black public schools reflected these dismal conditions and years of discrimination and neglect.

Although the stories of African American oppression in the segregated South should continue to be passionately and frequently taught to both African American and white educators and their students, this chapter is not a lamentation about low self-esteem, inferior physical facilities, poorly trained teachers, or white students' discarded books. My unusual story is about how a small number of African American students achieved and prospered in an all-Black Catholic school in the South, Mother Mary Mission. I am a non-Catholic who attended this all-Black, southern, segregated Catholic school administered by white priests and

 ISBN 0-8077-3530-2 (cloth).

nuns from the Midwest. This chapter explores the details of the curious mix of racial, religious, and school variables by focusing on one theme that is, I believe, pertinent and instructive—the resilience and adaptability of African American children in handling contradictory and contentious worlds. I will discuss this theme by referring to tensions created by race, religion, and the school's curriculum.

After returning from military service in Germany, my parents enrolled me in the local public elementary school but decided a year later that the inadequate and crowded facilities and half-day school sessions could never prepare me or my two sisters for a world outside the provincial constraints of our existing environment. Consequently, the only choice was to stretch their modest income and pay the tuition and fees so that we could attend the local Catholic school.

Mother Mary Mission Catholic School was an elementary and secondary school founded in 1941 by the Vincentian Sisters of Charity of Pittsburgh and the Salvatorian Fathers of Milwaukee. The name "Mission" was an appropriate designation; we often joked that the priests and nuns came to Alabama to teach Black children because they lacked the intestinal fortitude to become real African missionaries. Incidentally, I noticed on a recent visit that the school's name had been changed from Mother Mary Mission School to Mother Mary School.

RACE

A source of great tension for the students of this school was the fact that we were taught by white priests and nuns in a legal system of strict segregation. Unlike Catholic schools in neighboring Louisiana, where there was a Catholic African American presence and Black nuns, there were few Black or white Catholics in Alabama. Although our white teachers were obviously aware of the racial differences, they never acknowledged our African American heritage except for the one statue in the courtyard of the Black saint, Martin de Poores, to whom a few references were made, and the singing of an occasional spiritual during music classes. I cannot remember even one instance in which the religious teachers, who knew we were subjected to harsh treatment and inequities outside of home and school, ever explicitly addressed the issue of racism. We were treated as if we were simply dark-skinned white children in need of salvation.

Ironically, Catholics operated segregated schools in the South, never questioning or defying the assumptions that Black children should not be taught in the same classroom with white children. Whether this circumstance presented a moral dilemma to these nuns and priests is a question of great interest to me.

RELIGION

Another source of contention had to do with religious differences. As a child, I practiced two religions—the faith of the African Methodist Episcopal (AME) Church and Roman Catholicism. Although I was not Catholic and neither were 99% of the 250 students, I attended mass and catechism classes five days a week in school and weekly AME Sunday school classes, church services, and youth group meetings. Although our teachers told us that we would all burn in hell if we did not convert to Catholicism, few converted. My family has a long and distinguished history of leadership in the AME Church, and the family was unrelenting in its refusal to let me or my sisters convert to Catholicism. My grandmother succintly and poignantly summed up the family's position on this matter: She frequently reminded the family that "we got our ways and them Catholics got theirs."

So with much grace and fluidity, we watched private Catholic confessions and public AME testimonials. We admired the Catholic father and our Protestant preacher. Latin masses and altar boys' prayers were no problem; neither were spirituals and revivals. We unabashedly interacted with white nuns in black habits as well as Black ushers in white uniforms. I am amazed how well we, as small children, mastered this fine art of cultural switching. Bennett (1990) reinforces this observation by pointing out that children can "retain much of their original culture yet be multicultural at the same time" (p. 18). She explains that people are, in fact, capable of "multiple ways of perceiving, believing, doing, and evaluating so that they can conform to those aspects of the macroculture that are necessary for positive societal interaction, without eroding identification with their own ethnicity" (p. 18).

CURRICULUM

The curriculum at Mother Mary Mission was very different from the curriculum of the Black public schools. It was obvious to us, even as children, that the African American children in public schools were not exposed to the same quality curriculum that we were; so most of us never shared our Catholic school experiences and knowledge with our public school friends. We were different, and the difference was often stressful and uncomfortable. For example, in spite of our ability to switch easily from standard English to dialect, there were many instances in which Mother Mary Mission students were ridiculed by public school children for "talking like white folks."

We were exposed to a richer and broader curriculum than students in segregated public schools. Mother Mary Mission students took music classes for 12 years and were exposed to major European and white American classical compositions, as well as some African American spirituals. All students took four years of high school math and science as well as language classes in French, Spanish, Latin, or Greek. One of my most memorable experiences was the arrival of Father Austin Martin, who opened the world of theater to me through the work of playwrights such as Shakespeare and Moliere. We constantly recited poetry as well as lengthy biblical and literary passages, we diagramed sentences, and we spent endless evenings doing homework. Nevertheless, these grueling learning activities instilled in us a love of literature, music, and poetry. Interestingly, several of us wrote poems and essays that were published in national high school literary magazines.

This classical, "no-frills" curriculum excluded subjects such as home economics, shop, typing, and Alabama history. African American children of varying abilities, social classes, aspirations, and motivation had access to a superior college prep curriculum that was unavailable to our Black and white public school peers. Mother Mary Mission students benefited from our teachers' national and international perspectives. Unlike the public school teachers of Black and white children in the South, these nuns and priests had lived, studied, and traveled in diverse and multicultural settings. Father Gregory had studied in Rome and the eccentric Father Romuald, our history teacher, had a Ph.D. from a European university and is the author of a seminal book on Cardinal Newman. The nuns were similarly trained, although their experiences were shared with the students primarily within the context of religious discussions or proselytizing. For example, we learned about Mexico in the context of Our Lady of Guadalupe, Italy through reference to St. Francis of Assisi. These mission-oriented teachers believed that armed with proper schooling, hard work, discipline, and, of course, the Catholic faith, African American children could achieve and overcome the obstacles of hundreds of years of segregation. Any disobedience or resistance by students to the priests' and nuns' mission resulted in swift and often cruel penalties, including long periods of kneeling, public ridicule, and corporal punishment. My sisters and I were the victims of much of this punishment, since we were uniformily referred to as "the smart Jordan girls with bad attitudes."

I specifically remember an incident in elementary school in which my sister Jennifer was unjustly accused by one of the nuns' light-skinned Catholic favorites of calling the principal a "cockeyed bull frog." The charge was so ridiculous not because my sister was incapable of hurling diatribes but because her vocabulary, even as a child, was much more sophisticated and descriptive. The principal, Sister Mildred, demanded that my sister kneel in the doorway of the church as we exited, and she then accompanied her to each classroom in the school, where she had to apologize for an offense that she had not committed. The hurt and humiliation that my sisters and I experienced as a result of this injustice will never be forgotten.

Either unmindful of or unfettered by the fact that Black children in the South had few career options (either attend an all-Black college to become teachers, nurses, or ministers or work as domestics or mill workers), these white religious teachers persisted in their work. Many of us enrolled in colleges, and some even matriculated in Salvatorian colleges and seminaries. There is no question that many of us benefited from this strenuous and unusual curriculum. For those classmates who could not escape the confines of Phenix City, the anomaly of the college bound curriculum must have been even more curious.

IMPLICATIONS

I believe my past experiences have relevance to the present education of African American children. First, there was more cultural match than mismatch in this school. In the second chapter of my work, *Black Students and School Failure* (Irvine, 1990), I discuss the concept of cultural synchronism. I contend that the lack of cultural synchronization between African American students' homes/communities and their school is a major factor contributing to school failure. Often, the culture of minority students or their "way of life" (Ogbu, 1988) is incongruous with the white, middle-class cultural norms and behaviors of our schools. The differences result in cultural discontinuity, or lack of cultural synchronization, between the student and the school.

Furthermore, I say when there is a cultural mismatch or cultural incompatibility between students and their school, there are inevitable consequences: miscommunication; confrontations between minority students, the teacher, and the home; hostility; alienation; diminished self-esteem; and eventual school failure (Irvine, 1990).

Though this chapter discusses tension caused by lack of cultural synchronization and cultural mismatch, I believe that my experiences did not result in school failure for two reasons. The first reason is that there was more "match" than "mismatch" of cultures than was obvious to me as a child. For definitional purposes, culture is the total of ways of living (Hoopes & Pusch, 1979), a way of life that is shared by members of a population (Ogbu, 1988). Culture (Owens, 1987) is what one thinks is important (values), what one thinks is true (beliefs), and how one perceives how things are done (norms).

The essential conflict of my school experiences centers, I believe, on differences in norms more than values and beliefs. What the Catholic nuns and priests shared with my parents and the African American community were strong and dogmatic beliefs in the power of education over oppression and discrimination and values such as discipline, resilience, achievement, and hard work. There was a shared common mission and vision that was clearly articulated and passionately executed. My parents were more insistent upon my school success than the zealous nuns and priests; my father was more punitive regarding failure. Although I was told that the Catholics were misguided in their religious perspectives, they were to be respectfully tolerated because they held the key to our educational future. This belief in education served as the common foundation that minimized the potential for hostility and alienation between the African American Protestant community and the Catholic school. The Catholics, with their different religion, dress, ethnicity, and geographic origin, did not maintain an oppositional relationship with the African American children and their families.

More important, like our parents and the Black community that supported and pushed me, the Catholics believed that African American students could learn and achieve. This small but significant point ran counter to prevailing mythology that African American children were destined to a life of failure and inferiority. There was no cultural incompatibility on this point. No subject was considered too difficult, esoteric, or irrelevant. I was aware of the great financial sacrifices and emotional disturbances my parents experienced to keep us in Catholic school, so I mastered the curriculum and kept my rebellious outbreaks to a minimum.

Second, the African American community, primarily through the AME Church, provided the cultural centeredness and historical foundation for my development. The Catholic school was not expected to perform this racial socialization function. The task was too important to be left to individuals outside the immediate family/community. It was in the African American community and the family that we were taught the means to survive the taunts, insults, and debasement of the racist white community. In fact, we were taught that racists were ignorant people who were beneath us in status and native intellectual ability. We knew the history of African Americans—such as our heroes, songs, poems, rituals, games.

Our importance and responsibility to the community at large was emphasized. I consider this third point to be most critical. During my childhood in the South, African American children were the center of all activities. We were praised lavishly by our parents, as well as by church and community members, for our accomplishments; we were encouraged and bolstered during failures. Individual achievements became opportunities for community celebrations. Finally, we thought that the survival of the race depended on our courage, commitment, and resolve. We were frequently drilled on the importance of education and excellence in the struggle for justice and equality. It was not unusual that African American children during this era believed that improved race relations and racial equality were related to our individual achievement and performance.

I have emphasized this second point because of the recent emotional debate about the importance of an Afrocentric curriculum for African American children. My educational autobiography raises questions: Should this important task of cultural and historical centeredness be delegated to state-run schools and their functionaries? Should this racial socialization process be left exclusively to the African American community and family? If some African American families are unable or unwilling to assume this role, can schools perform the necessary tasks without the family's support? How can the schools and African American communities forge new partnerships in the 1990s based on a shared mission and common visions?

Third, the school and its classroom were small; there were approximately 250 students in grades 1 through 12. The school I attended was incredibly small and intimate. The average graduating class at Mother Mary Mission School was 25. Research indicates that in 1989, 70% of urban elementary schools had enrollments of more than 300 students (Polite, 1992), although data suggest that students prosper in smaller schools rather than larger ones. The school and the community populations were stable, and the African American families knew each other. Many of my classmates' parents had attended school with my mother, and our family name was well known in the community.

I have no inclination to romanticize my past or sentimentalize my past educational experiences. Growing up in Alabama in the 1950s and 1960s was very difficult and painful. This chapter is not a call for Catholic education for all African American children or a call for a revival of the Protestant ethic in Black communities. Instead, it is the intent of this chapter to provide some insight into how one African American family, a supportive church and community, and a unique Catholic school sheltered children from the psychological despair and an inferior education inherent in an evil system of racial segregation. My educational history suggests that in spite of institutional systems designed to oppress African Americans, there were and continue to be resourceful and committed families who find the means to provide a quality education for their children.

REFERENCES

Bennett, C. I. (1990). *Comprehensive multicultural education* (2nd ed.). Boston: Allyn & Bacon.

Hoopes, D. S., & Pusch, M. D. (1979). Definitions of terms. In M. D. Pusch (Ed.), *Multicultural education: A cross-cultural training approach* (pp. 2–8). Yarmouth, ME: Intercultural Press.

Irvine, J. J. (1990). *Black students and school failure: Policies, practices, and prescriptions.* Westport, CT: Greenwood.

Ogbu, J. (1988). Cultural diversity and human development. In D. T. Slaughter (Ed.), *Black children and poverty: A developmental perspective* (pp. 11–28). San Francisco: Jossey-Bass.

Owens, R. G. (1987). *Organizational behavior in education.* Englewoods Cliffs, NJ: Prentice Hall.

Polite, V. C. (1992). Getting the job done well: African Americans in Catholic schools. *Journal of Negro Education, 61*, 211–222.

CHAPTER 6

Mea Culpa, Mea Culpa, Mea Maxima Culpa: The French Catholic School Experience

Michèle Foster

There is considerable discussion about the kind of experiences necessary to assist minority students in becoming successful in the school setting. In a recent *Educational Researcher* article, Ogbu (1992) identifies two competing approaches currently being advocated in the contemporary school reform movements. The first is the core curriculum and the second, multicultural education. For those who may not have read Ogbu's article, let me briefly review each. According to Ogbu, the core curriculum approach, one advocated by E. D. Hirsch, Jr., and Allan Bloom, calls for all students to study a common core curriculum. The multicultural approach includes multiple approaches ranging from multicultural education for cross-cultural understanding, culturally responsive education or pedagogy, bilingual and bicultural education, cultural pluralism, and various other approaches.

If one were to fit the education provided by Catholic schools into one of these two categories, it would have to fall into that of a common core curriculum. In fact, much of the success of Catholic schools is attributed to their emphasis on the basics, a core curriculum that all students are expected to take and master (Coleman, 1981).

According to Ogbu, however, neither of these approaches alone is likely to enhance the school achievement of certain minority groups because they fail to take into account what he considers to be the more important and larger ecological issues—the historical, social and economic relationship between various minority groups and the larger society—that influence a minority group's school success. Ogbu's ecological perspective classifies African Americans as involuntary minorities, castelike groups whose historical economic and social position relative to larger society more or less determines their schooling outcomes.

Much of the criticism of Ogbu's perspective hinges on its failure to account for the different experiences that characterize individuals and families who belong to particular groups of involuntary minorities. Only recently I have begun to systematically examine my experiences of growing up in a small New England town and attending a French Catholic school in light of the various paradigms I encountered during graduate school. In so doing, I have come to realize that, though Ogbu's model would classify my family as an involuntary minority, my particular familial, community, and schooling experiences placed me more in the category of the voluntary minorities who have achieved school success using the strategy Gibson (1988) calls "accommodation without assimilation." I offer my own story as a counterexample to Ogbu's model that assigns particular groups to static categories based on the group's particular historical, social, and economic relationship to the larger society. It is my hope that this example might provide a case that demonstrates how, rather than being static, environmental and situational influences interact in a way that can result in particular families adopting strategies that are believed to be more characteristic of those of other types of minority groups.

Unlike the stories of Irvine (Chapter 5) and Delpit (Chapter 8), which are anchored in the segregated South of pre-*Brown*, mine takes place during the same era but in the North, in Marlboro, Massachusetts, a small New England town not unlike Great Barrington, where W.E.B. DuBois resided. There is a tendency to ignore the experiences of individuals who grew up in such environments. However, it is important to remember that the failure to examine these atypical experiences will result in an incomplete understanding of the experiences of African Americans.

When I was born in 1947, Marlboro, although incorporated under a city charter, was a small New England town of 16,000. Founded in 1660, Marlboro is situated 30 miles east of Boston and some 15 miles west of Worcester, two of the largest cities in Massachusetts at the time. Populated by a small number of Yankees and an even smaller number of Jews, it was principally a working-class town, home to a variety of white ethnic groups, the majority of whom were Catholic and lived in particular ethnic enclaves.

A Catholic church and parochial school, the focal point of each neighborhood, defined each neighborhood, which was inseparable from the parish. St. Anne's parish, the church, and its parochial school, situated in the west end of town, served the predominantly Italian American population. The church offered sermons in Italian, and the children studied both

English and Italian in the school. The Immaculate Conception parish was located in the downtown section right off Main Street. At the Immaculate Conception church and in its parochial school, which we called the Irish school, students studied only English. St. Marie's Catholic church and its parochial school, St. Antoine's, later renamed St. Marie's when a new brick school building was added, was located in French Hill.

French Hill, the area where my family lived, was home to the majority of Marlboro's large French Canadian population. My family had lived in the French Hill area of Marlboro since 1857, when Luke Goins, my great-great grandfather, the first relative on my mother's side that my family knew of, fled slavery in Harpers Ferry, at that time in Virginia but now West Virginia, to Marlboro, where he built a house and raised 12 children; my grandmother was the first of his grandchildren.

Though my mother had married and gone to live with my father in Hartford, Connecticut, his hometown, she returned to her childhood home in Marlboro when her marriage ended. Thus I grew up in an extended family made up of my mother and maternal grandparents in a house that had been built by my maternal great-great grandfather and in which my great-grandmother, my grandmother, and mother had been raised.

It was within my family and local community that I learned my first lessons about being simultaneously both an insider and an outsider. These lessons helped me learn to accommodate to the demands of the larger society without being fully assimilated. Being both an insider and outsider in the small, predominantly white New England community where my family had lived since 1857 necessitated not only that I understand the values of mainstream Anglo culture but also become proficient in its norms and behaviors. It was not only household and community circumstances that dictated these lessons, but also my family's expressed desire for me to prepare myself to take advantage of the improved opportunities for Blacks they believed were on the horizon. My grandparents' recollections gave me access to my family's historical, social, and economic circumstances that furnished a broader view of my lineage and my place in it than I could have envisioned on my own. At the same time, however, my family wanted me to have a strong racial identity, to feel at ease and be part of the African American community in which we spent the most significant portion of our social lives. Consequently, they expected me to recognize when the values of the separate but overlapping communities were at odds and, depending on the context, to demonstrate appropriate behaviors. Whether taught explicitly by noting where specific transgressions had occurred or more indirectly through family stories, the lessons were unambiguous and unequivocal. For instance, because of my early school success and the prospect of a favorable future in academic pursuits, my mother made sure I internalized the lessons that while scholarly pursuits were important they were not more important than nor were they to override competence in social interaction. One could never retreat to solitary activities like reading or practicing the piano, which I sometimes did, if others desired social interaction. To do so was considered rude and self-centered and acting white. Another lesson drilled into me was the African American prohibition against boasting and self-aggrandizement, behaviors commonly associated with the white community, which my family openly scorned. It was not uncommon to hear the sarcastic retort, "That's damn white of you," addressed to someone for calling attention to some act generally expected of them. Correspondingly, it was not unusual for a person who had been complimented for some personal achievement to minimize its importance by responding, "White folks raised me."

In order to establish the fact that our family was both insider and outsider, and to reinforce a responsibility to fight all injustices, my grandmother told many stories. One of her favorites described an incident that occurred when my uncle was a teenager. While walking with friends, all white, on the way home from school one day, he was verbally attacked by a group of out-of-towners, who were in town to work on a construction project. A person who rarely tolerated insults of any kind, my grandmother insisted that the town fathers take action. The mayor along with other city officials responded by demanding that the crew leave town "by sundown." Outsiders, they insisted, could not harass any of the townspeople.

While this story can be read as an acknowledgment of my family's insider status, my grandmother told other stories that highlighted our family's position as outsiders. In one story, my grandmother recalled the fierce battle she had undertaken to insure that my mother and uncle were placed in the high school college preparatory program instead of the vocational track deemed more suitable to the employment prospects for Negroes, as they were called in the 1940s. Accompanying my grandmother's stories were my grandfather's and mother's stories. My grandfather liked to recall his early involvement in founding of the Brotherhood of Sleeping Car Porters. His charter membership certificate in one of the first unions to wage a collective struggle for fair treatment of Black workers hung prominently in our living room. He often said that the only group more radical than the Brotherhood of Sleeping Car Porters was the Black communists. When I was in college, my mother, a registered nurse who had trained at the Harlem School of Nursing, refused to let me donate blood to the Red Cross because she remembered when that agency used to take donations of blood from Blacks and pour them down the sink rather than contaminate the blood of whites with Black blood. And I remember being slightly embarrassed when she wrote a letter stating as much to the college president who had made the request.

While the perception of limited opportunity can result in developing an oppositional frame of reference with respect to academic achievement (Ogbu, 1992) or developing a "raceless persona" in order to achieve academically (Fordham, 1988), my family's response to any perception of limited opportunity was to excel in spite of the limitations and to maintain strong cultural and political affiliations and ties to the Black community in the process. In other words, my family strove to make sure that I would develop what DuBois (1903) referred to as a "double consciousness," to know who I was and what I was capable of achieving regardless of the prevailing beliefs of society.

Consequently, by the time I began kindergarten at the local parochial French Catholic school in 1952, my family's personal experiences as insiders and outsiders would assist me in coping with the cultural discontinuities that I would confront throughout my schooling experiences, in discerning the cultural continuities and cultural discontinuities, and in choosing among the various strategic options. In 1954, the year I began second grade at St. Anne's Academy, the school had been in existence for 65 years. St. Anne's Academy, or Académie Sainte-Anne as it was known in French, was founded by the Sisters of St. Anne, an order whose motherhouse was in Lachine, Canada, in the province of Québec. A teaching order, the Sisters of St. Anne had established and had run parochial and boarding schools in Canada and in the United States for students from Francophone communities. In addition to schools in Canada and the United States, their missionary work also included maintaining a school in Haiti.

In the United States their schools were located in the French Canadian communities of New England: in the Rhode Island communities of Woonsocket and Pawtucket; and in the Massachusetts communities of Attleboro, Lowell, Lawrence, Worcester, Webster, Fitchburg, and North Adams. In each of these locations, their schools aimed to provide students with a bilingual education designed to enable them to maintain their ethnic ties to their communities. To that end, the instruction provided throughout elementary school was bilingual. Both St. Antoine's, later renamed St. Marie's parochial school and St. Anne's Academy, the French academy, were staffed by the Sisters of St. Anne.

St. Anne's Academy was one of the centerpieces of the order's schools. Unlike its parochial schools, St. Anne's was a single-sex school, which included second grade through high school. And the mission of the school included not only a bilingual education but a classical one as well. The purpose of the school was threefold: (1) to help young women discover their religious vocations; (2) to provide the kind of experiences to young women who chose a married vocation that would enable them to be good Catholic wives and mothers; and (3) to provide students with the background necessary to enter Catholic women's colleges in New England (including Anna Maria College, a Catholic women's college founded by the order) or elsewhere in the United States.

To meet these goals, the program offered at the Academy included six years (second through eighth grade) of bilingual education, with courses taught in French by a nun who was a native speaker of the language and courses taught in English by a nun whose first language was English. Elementary school subjects offered in English included history, geography, science, mathematics, reading, spelling, penmanship, music, catechism, and art. Subjects taught in French included dictation (*dictée*), spelling, reading, catechism, and, after third grade, the formal study of French grammar. In addition to French and English subjects, beginning in seventh grade all students were required to take six years of secular Latin, which reinforced the religious Latin prayers we had memorized since second grade. In addition to the Latin begun in seventh grade and religion begun in grammar school, high school subjects included four years of French, four years of English, four years of math through trigonometry, four years of science through physics, four years of history, and, beginning in eleventh grade, two years of classical Greek. All Academy students studied an instrument until they demonstrated a certain level of competence in both theory and performance. We took art—history and studio—until we demonstrated a certain level of proficiency in charcoal, pastels, and oil painting. Physical education, typing, sewing and cooking, and participation in organized intramural sports made up the rest of the program. In order to keep us busy, a full complement of extracurricular activities was available, including varsity sports, the secular or religious choir, work on the student newspaper, student government, the yearbook, math club, science club, the National Honor Society, and Sodality, a religious organization.

The nuns believed that all the subjects and a full complement of extracurricular activities were essential for young women whether they were contemplating the religious life, a vocation as wife and mother, or entrance into a Catholic women's college.

The program I had just described may seem impossible to implement because of time constraints, but at the Academy such a program was possible because the school had been founded as a boarding school.

When I entered the school as a second grader in 1954, the number of students enrolled at the Academy in grades 2–12 was 280, with approximately 80 day students and 200 boarders. Not until 1963, one year before my graduation from high school, did the number of day students approximate the number of boarding students. In that year the total number of students had peaked at 340, with 160 day students and 180 boarders. Students at the Academy attended school from 8 A.M. until 4:30 P.M. daily and from 8:00 A.M. until noon on Saturdays.

While there were several ways in which my school experiences represented cultural and social discontinuities and cast me in the role of outsider, there were many other ways in which these experiences overlapped with my own family experiences and worked to include me as an insider. Let me discuss three that are rooted in issues of language, ethnicity and race, religion, and performance.

LANGUAGE, ETHNICITY, AND RACE

One of the obvious differences between me and my classmates was the fact that most of them were white. They were not only white, but French Canadian, and the majority had grandparents or parents who had immigrated to the United States from Francophone Canada. When I reached high school, Haitian students—some from Haiti, others from New York—entered the school as boarders. These were the first students with whom I shared a common racial, if not ethnic, identity.

The prominence of the students' Francophone background was evident in the day-to-day life of the Academy. Not only were we enrolled in bilingual classes, but the everyday language of the school—on the playground, during recess, in conversations among peers, during lunch—was French. In fact, a recurring phrase that was often heard in these settings was "Un jeton, s'il-vous-plait" ("a token, please"), directed at a student who had been overheard speaking English. Every day, we stood and recited, "Je jure allégiance au drapeau des États Unies d'Amerique," the opening line of the pledge of allegiance in French, a pledge that most of us were only able to recite in French. Every year, students who performed exceptionally well in French classes were selected to participate in the Congrès de la Langue Française held in Canada, which in 1954 the Academy even had the honor of hosting.

Because many of the students spoke Franco American French or the version of French characteristic of Haiti, the nuns, while they never insisted on Parisian French, could often be heard reminding students that a particular word or phrase was not school French, but rather the French to be spoken within the confines of family, neighborhood, and home community. Because I spoke only one version of French, I did not have to cope with these discontinuities between home and school language. But I could easily compare that admonition with my own delicate balancing act of knowing when to use standard English and when to use African American English. Having the opportunity to witness other students struggling to keep the language of school separate from that of community and family was comforting.

In my case, the nuns often told me that while I was not French Canadian or Haitian, there was no reason not to speak fluent French. After all, they pointed out, in Haiti and in Africa people just like me spoke French. To encourage me to claim French as my own and to link me to the Caribbean and Africa, I was the student who, when we were visited by distinguished visitors (usually clergy from Africa or the Caribbean), made presentations in French and English. I remember presenting a bouquet of flowers to Monseigneur J. Kiwanuka, Vicar Apostolic of Uganda, and greeting Emmanul Mabathoan, the Bishop of Leribe Basutoland, with the phrase, "a moi toute petite fleure Africaine," which in English translates to "for me, a little African flower."

While I make no claim that the nuns' view of me was not tinged by racism, the constant reminders of my African origins worked to make me feel at ease using a language that I could not claim as my birthright by linking me to other Blacks with whom I could share another language. And this was long before I knew anything about pan-Africanism or the diaspora of Blacks.

RELIGION

One of the distinguishing features of Saint Anne's was its emphasis on religion. Not only did we study catechism and learn French, English, and Latin version of prayers, but religion permeated the school environment. The third floor of the Academy contained the sisters' cloister; the sisters' refectory (cafeteria) was across from ours, where everyday we witnessed the sisters filing out of their refectory after lunch reciting the Angelus, a noon prayer, while on their way to the chapel on the second floor. Across the street from the Academy was the order's novitiate, and as students we not only saw the postulants and novices on a daily basis, but also got to witness the yearly investiture of new novices.

All students were expected to participate in the ritual activities of the Catholic Church; a chapel occupied one wing of the school. Liturgical activities included the annual procession for the feast of Corpus Christi and the annual procession in honor of Mary Immaculate, to name but two. There were also special years dedicated specifically to particular religious events; 1954, the Marian Year, was devoted entirely to special religious activities honoring the Virgin Mary. That year Academy students donned special light blue jumpers and white blouses for particular religious events, such as the singing of the "Ave Maria" for the Offertory at the Cathedral of the Holy Cross in Boston, the pilgrimage to LaSallette Shrine in Attleboro, and the crowning of the imposing statue of the Blessed Virgin Mary erected at the entrance to our campus.

Boarding students were encouraged to rise early to attend morning mass and to engage in other activities that would facilitate their discovery of a religious vocation and prepare them for that experience.

All the students, including those from Haiti, were Catholic. The fact that I was not Catholic highlighted my role as outsider. Although nominally Protestant, except for an occasional visit to the Black Baptist Church in Worcester, my family did not attend church on a regular basis. Nonetheless, like every other student, I memorized catechism, attended mass and other religious ceremonies, sang Gregorian chant, prayed in Latin, English, and French, recited the altar boy's responses to the priests' prayers, watched as my classmates received the sacraments—went to confession, made their first Holy Communions, and were confirmed—and hoped that I would go to limbo instead of hell as the nuns preached that those who were unbaptized would.

My family thought religious training was important for children. The primary purpose of religion, as they saw it was the reinforcement of the moral training received at home, not the distinctive articles of faith. Consequently, the particular denomination was unimportant. When they disagreed with some of the religious teachings being promulgated, as they sometimes did, they actively sought to counter them. For instance, because we were New Englanders, we had adopted the custom of eating fish on Friday. There were times, however, when the family ate meat on Friday, and my mother and grandparents refused to let me repeat the prohibitions about eating meat on Friday in their house. More than anything, my family worried about what they considered to be the strange ideas about sexuality and childbearing that they believed the nuns promulgated, and they actively worked to disabuse me of these ideas.

PERFORMANCE

One of the hallmarks of the Academy was the emphasis it placed on public performances. The religious and secular choir sang regularly. At least twice a year, the nuns mounted plays. They staged elaborate performances for religious and secular holidays as well as to mark the opening and closing of school. Music students gave yearly recitals. Elementary and high school graduations, designed to be aesthetically pleasing, always included poetry and music.

My own earliest family experiences had included public performances. My grandmother, an ex-showgirl who had danced in the Black Broadway musicals of the 1920s, ran a dancing school in the town. Throughout my childhood, she participated in summer stock and light opera performances. And desirous of a stage career for me, she inducted me into show business at an early age. At 12 months I had donned dancing shoes and begun taking dancing lessons in her studio. By the time I began school, I had appeared in several summer stock performances, cut a record, been a featured performer at local policemen's balls, appeared on the "Ted Mack Amateur Hour," been Miss Fire Prevention of Worcester, and been interviewed on local radio programs. All of these experiences were nurtured at St. Anne's, with its tradition of elaborate performances.

CONCLUSION

The nuns did nothing to mitigate any discontinuities—cultural, religious, or linguistic—between my own background and that of the other students or the school curriculum. They left that task up to my family. Moreover, much of the Academy's curriculum and the pedgagogical practices used to teach are probably considered unenlightened by contemporary standards. After all, we were taught to read using the look-and-say method, we read in round-robin fashion, spent hours diagraming sentences, and, with the aid of mnemonic devices, memorizing seemingly useless information. But somehow, despite these misguided efforts, the nuns managed to teach us. A large part of their effectiveness was because the nuns took seriously their responsibility to teach all their pupils, including the Black ones. My mother used to say that she thought the nuns were the ideal teachers because they believed if their students failed to learn, they (the nuns, not the students) would go to hell. Since the nuns believed in hell and didn't want to go there, my mother concluded that this was the best motivation.

As I consider these experiences retrospectively, especially in light of my own research with exemplary African American teachers, I have discovered some important similarities. First is that, like the teachers I have been studying, these nuns espoused an ideology, a belief that all students could be successful academically and master the curricular offerings, whatever they were. Because they believed in their own self-efficacy and subscribed to the belief that effort, not ability, produced achievement, they were tough, demanding, and insistent on quality performance. When I consider all my educational experiences, from kindergarten through graduate school, my years at the local parochial school and at the Academy were the only educational institutions where these convictions held sway and were acted upon.

Compared to today's contemporary menu of curricular choices and pedagogical practices, the diet practiced by the nuns may seem inadequate. Despite any inadequacies, this diet possessed one essential element—a belief in the educability of students, confidence in their skills, and a commitment to educating all students—that is lacking today.

REFERENCES

Coleman, J. (1981). Quality and equality in American education: Public and Catholic. *Phi Delta Kappan, 63,* 59–164.

DuBois, W. E. B. (1903). *The souls of Black folk.* Greenwich, CT: Fawcett.

Fordham, S. (1988). Racelessness as a factor in Black students' success: Pragmatic strategy or Pyrrhic victory? *Harvard Educational Review, 58*(1), 29–84.

Gibson, M. (1988). *Accommodation without assimilation: Sikh immigrants in an American high school.* Ithaca, NY: Cornell University Press.

Ogbu, J. (1992, November). Understanding cultural diversity and learning. *Educational Researcher,* pp. 5–14, 24.

5

A Good Education and the Fear of God

Mary E. Dilworth

African Americans, possibly more so than others, place a high premium on religion and education. Both have contributed to the survival of our people through immensely arduous times and conditions. Both are perceived as critical to a better quality of life on earth and in the hereafter. Although strong religious faith and its tenets—such as discipline, integrity, and devotion to good works—complement academic achievement, it is essential that educators and parents translate the relationship between religion and education in a manner that prepares students for the trials and tribulations of this diverse and complex society.

Racial, ethnic, and linguistic cultural responsiveness, currently recognized as important in teaching practice in all schools, is particularly important in the parochial school environment. In parochial schools, learning occurs within another culture—a religious one—that is often more removed from the students' community than in public schools. While students in parochial schools are typically offered exemplary learning conditions, they are also in greater need than public school students of guidance as they learn to negotiate the outside world.

I contend that the dilemma for African American parents, and other parents with options, is to find a parochial school with the appropriate balance of academic, spiritual, and cultural presence that engages their children in a culturally responsive manner. In the absence of cultural responsiveness in parochial schools, African American parents are compelled to orchestrate a home and community experience that supplements that which is absent in the school. This was the challenge that many African Americans faced as they attempted to raise well-rounded, educated, and happy children in Catholic schools. This chapter chronicles the story of my parents' efforts, and those of countless others, to do so.

In search of a better life, my parents moved from New York City to nearby Plainfield, New Jersey, when I was about 3 years old. The community of Plainfield, with a population of approximately 48,000, was a typical northeastern suburb of the 1950s and 1960s. Often first- and second-generation European immigrant families had fathers who were veterans of World War II or the Korean conflict and mothers who worked at home. Approximately 22% of the population was nonwhite. Numerous job opportunities were almost equally split between white-collar and blue-collar work, with many of the white-collar jobs 40 minutes away in New York City and the blue-collar jobs in nearby manufacturing companies ranging from a Mack Truck plant to Johnson & Johnson Pharmaceuticals.

My mother worked at home caring for my three sisters, my brother, and me. Although he worked part-time as an upholsterer, my father's primary job was as a shipping clerk for a small chain company, and we lived conveniently in a spacious apartment above the office where he worked. The office was situated in the downtown area, and, as a result, we were somewhat isolated from the two small pockets of African Americans on the far west and east ends of town. My neighborhood playmates, who lived in one of three apartment buildings nearby, were as diverse as one would expect for the time. Most were Irish, Polish, and Italian American Catholics, with a few Jewish and Chinese American kids included.

My mother is from upstate New York, and my father is from Mississippi. Although a few relatives eventually followed my parents into central New Jersey, my parents had very few Black friends or relatives living in town. Their social life remained in New York City, and it seemed we traveled the 26 miles from Plainfield to New York almost every weekend. Neither of my parents had been raised as a Roman Catholic; however, I do not recall any of their Methodist roots evidenced in our home. As best I recall, it was strictly Catholic—fish sticks or tuna casserole was our Friday night cuisine. My mother, influenced by an aunt she had lived with in New York City after high school, had converted then, and my father converted later, when I was in elementary school. They married on Valentine's Day in a Bronx rectory. I am their oldest child and was baptized in the Catholic Church.

At 5 years old, I was enrolled in the kindergarten of St. Mary's School, according to my parents, for the same two reasons that all four of my siblings attended Catholic school: (1) for a good basic education (my parents questioned the quality of the neighborhood public school) and (2) to put the fear of God into us. A clear understanding of right and wrong and a mastery of the "King's English" were essentials of success in their view.

St. Mary's School was similar to most northeastern Catholic schools and churches of the time. It was very large, very crowded, and ethnically segregated. In our community, there were three parishes to choose from: St. Mary's, which was predominantly Irish; St. Bernard's, which was predominantly Italian; and St. Stanislas, which was predominantly Polish. St. Mary's parish, the largest and oldest of the three, was located on the west end of town, closest to our home. My years at St. Mary's, and subsequently at St. Bernard's, were happy ones, and rarely did it occur to me that my siblings and I were any different from the other students. The fact that from grades K–6, I was the only noticeable Black student in my class of approximately 150 students (divided among three rooms) eluded me.

In the second grade, a new girl arrived from Italy who, as I recall, spoke very little English. We were in the same class through fifth grade, but it was not until the sixth grade that, to my surprise, I learned her father was African American. We eventually became good friends and attended public high school and the same historically Black college together. On transferring in the sixth grade to a new Catholic school, I joined one other African American girl who had been the sole minority presence in her class for a number of years.

We were taught by Sisters of Charity in St. Mary's School and by Sisters of St. John the Baptist in St. Bernard's School. It appeared to me, as a child, that the teachers showed absolutely no discrimination in issuing praise or punishment. As I recall, all of us prayed every hour at the bell, wrote "Jesus, Mary, and Joseph" ("JMJ") at the top of every work paper, and made the sign of the cross each time we passed a Catholic church. We were *all* rapped on the knuckles for dirty fingernails and severely chastised for turning in homework or worksheets with crossouts or eraser marks. It seemed that we all despised diagraming sentences—and the principal. In my color-blind mind, it all came down to whether you were good or bad, and I modestly say that I was good and thus progressed through elementary school excelling academically and feeling socially accepted by my peers.

Of course, what I once saw as normal through a child's eyes I now, as an adult, recognize as significantly noteworthy. As my parents will attest, there were those individuals who were less than thrilled to see Black Catholics or to see a Black child in Catholic school, and who were certainly annoyed to see a Black child amidst white students succeed or be recognized for that success.

My very first realization that I *may* have been different was in second or third grade when I found out that the entire class had been invited to a classmate's birthday party. Everyone, that is, except for me. Presuming this had been an oversight, I asked the birthday girl about it. She told me that she wanted to invite me but that her father told her that she could not. My mother then explained to me that some people just did not like Black people, and, in my young mind, that was enough of an answer. On the one hand, I was comfortable with this basic knowledge, knowing that it was the girl's father, not she, who disliked me. On the other hand, I was less comfortable with my classmates when we began to study the Civil War and slaves. I remember the textbook explaining in great detail not only that slaves were Negroes from Africa but also what Negroes looked like—"very dark skin," "tight curly hair." It seemed to me that each time the word "Negro" was spoken, the entire class would turn and look at me as if I physically verified the description or could attest to the atrocities of slavery. Indeed, when I returned to school after a sick day, a classmate told me that Sister had given them a lecture about me. I am not certain what she said, but apparently it worked because they stopped staring. Nevertheless, from that Civil War unit until my first college course on Black Power, I somehow felt as if I was carrying the load for an entire race of people, most of whom I did not even know.

My parents were always complimentary of my school achievements, so it was not unusual that my good report cards brought a broad smile to my father's face. I did not learn until years later that my dad had had a standing $5 bet with the father of a white classmate, with whom he worked, as to which one of us would get the better report card. Thus my academic achievement also consistently improved my father's finances. My father says that this brought him enormous pleasure month after month and year after year, as his puzzled colleague never won a bet.

A report card also brought me to another reality. Midyear fourth grade I received a terrible report card: P (poor) or F (fail) on nearly all subjects—including religion, which was arguably a mortal sin. My family was in a panic, and I was restricted from watching television, roller skating, and all other amenities. At the same time, a girl in my class who typically did poorly returned to school with $10 for her greatly improved report card. It never occurred to me to question why my grades were so low when I had done nothing different. One full month later, Sister called us to her desk and stated that she had made a mistake and transposed our grades. While my classmate was retained that year, I still did not feel compensated for the embarrassment that I had felt for that month, feeling as though I had done something terribly wrong, not knowing what to do differently, and, most importantly, lacking an apology from Sister. While it has since been pointed out to me that she may have just been an insensitive woman, I was convinced, at the time, that if the tables had been turned, a sincere apology would have been forthcoming. It was at this point that the notion that teachers, nuns in particular, were always right lost validity with me.

To the best of my knowledge, most Catholic school students become briefly devoted to the Church or even to the idea that they have a vocation to be a priest or a nun. As I recall, the idea of becoming a nun appealed to me for only an extremely brief period because, in my mother's opinion, 14 years old, the typical age to start pursuing such a vocation, was too young to make a life decision. Second, and most important, I never thought I was holy enough to get into a convent. Although my mother indicated that a few Black nuns and priests did exist—"somewhere in New York"—I had never seen any. However, the possibility that I would be denied acceptance in any Catholic religious order because I was Black never entered my mind.

Regardless of my suitability for religious life, when I was about 9 or 10 years old, I did spend quite a bit of time just hanging out around the church—helping to clean, attending 5:30 A.M. masses with 80- and 90-year-old ladies, going to novenas, and attending various programs offered by various sacred societies. It was at one of these events that I came to the conclusion that white people did not know much about Black people in general or about me in particular. It was a meeting of a missionary society at which a priest showed slides and spoke of all the poor pagans in a certain country in Africa. He solicited the support and the prayers of the group, and at the end they served punch and cookies. As I munched my snack, my very limited knowledge (specifically, assurances from my parents that all Jews and Protestants were not doomed) told me that all these African pagans were not going to hell, and I could not imagine what all these very old white ladies could do about it even if they were all going to live in eternity with Satan. I was thoroughly convinced that this particular missionary approach to salvation was a waste when one of the ladies came up to me and sincerely asked if I was from the African country. How absurd I thought—even if I did look to her like one of the pagans, how could I be at St. Mary's Church all the way from Africa without my parents?

I was too young to realize when I was actually representing my race and failed. Catholic parishes tend to pay special homage to the saints for whom they are named. St. Mary's was no exception. As students we were encouraged to pray to the Blessed Mother directly, as she most certainly had great and special influence over her Son. The month of May was devoted entirely to the Virgin Mother, with the major event being the crowning of her statue in the church. Literally hundreds of school children, dressed in their white holy communion or confirmation clothes, marched solemnly in procession through the streets to a celebration in the church. Needless to say, the name "Mary" was extremely popular, and while I have been assured that my name is more a matter of family tradition than religious fervor, it fits in neatly at any Catholic occasion.

One April day, just before lunch, the friendly, sixtyish, blue-eyed, pipe-smoking Monsignor, who was the highest authority for the parish and school, came to all three first-grade classes and asked each girl named Mary to step out into the hallway—there was a crowd of white girls and me. He scanned our group with a smile and then announced in his kindly voice that I would crown the Blessed Mother in the May procession. The fact that this was 1957, on the heels of the *Brown* decision and that I was, to the best of my knowledge, the only Black child in the school from grades K–5 did not occur to me. I reasoned that I had been picked because I had good grades.

As I recall, I was terrified on that day as I walked through the streets with a beautiful crown on a satin pillow followed by hundreds of children behind me. The church was filled to the rafters, and when it was time to crown the statue of the Blessed Mother, the elderly Monsignor picked me up from where I stood behind the statue. We were both shaking—he, from the weight of the child in his arms; I, from pure fright as I put the crown on her head. I watched in horror as it slid right off the front and crashed to the floor, a huge ruby flying across the altar. The statue rocked wildly in its prominent spot in front of the congregation, and I began to cry, my hands covering my face. My parents recount that they were inclined to run up and snatch me off the alter, as Monsignor should never have tried to pick me up at his age anyway—at the same time, they were calculating how much a statue of the Virgin Mary could possibly cost.

The older I got, the more I felt that I was carrying the reputation of the Negro race on my shoulders. Virtually every person old enough at the time to have reached the age of reason remembers where they were when John F. Kennedy was shot. Although this incident was indeed tragic, and shocking, to everyone, the news was delivered to us in a manner typical of the drama and ceremony that is prevalent in the Catholic religion. Our teacher received a buzz on the intercom and left the room; after a few moments, she returned and instructed the entire class to stand up, turn around to face the back of the classroom, kneel down, and close our eyes. For many of us, this was the finale to the many air-raid drills we had endured over the years—we knew we were getting ready to be bombed by the Russians! Instead, Sister announced that the president had been shot, and we began a series of prayers for his soul and for that of his assassin. I, for one, did what I was told, but I also added a very special prayer of thanks. Since Sister had not said the assassin was a Negro (as I am sure she would have mentioned), my people and I were spared what I knew would have been the wrath of the country, and my classmates, for what had happened to the first Roman Catholic president.

"You don't know your own people" was one of the most seemingly unjust but accurate statements that I can remember my mother offering to me at age 14 in justification for declaring that I would attend public high school. "If we lived in New York City it would be different, there would be more of us, and I don't care what Sister says, you are going to public high school!"

As I completed the eighth grade at St. Bernard's, there was immense pressure on me to continue a Catholic education by going to one of the two largely white Catholic high schools in the area: Union Catholic, a fairly new, coeducational institution established to accommodate the children of the working class, or the more exclusive all-girls high school, Mount Saint Mary's, sitting high on a hill in the scenic Watchung Mountains, but also overlooking the commercial thoroughfare of Route 22 with supermarkets, gas stations, and high-speed Chevrolets.

Throughout the school year, Sister would take a poll of how many of her students planned to attend Catholic high school. In the fall, about a half dozen of my classmates had indicated that they would not attend Catholic high school but, by spring, either their parents had given in to the pressure of the school faculty and clerics, or my classmates just lied. By graduation, I was one of only two students who were not going to parochial school, and Sister made it perfectly clear that we were messing up her record. My parents stood their ground, dismissing a scholarship offer and remaining confident that my brains would not melt away in public school, as was suggested by one of the faithful. My parents say that they were adamant about my attending public high school as a means of fulfilling their goal to have a happy, well-rounded child. Regardless of my outgoing personality, my parents were concerned that my teenage years would be a social disaster with few, if any, African American teenagers as classmates.

As I reflect back on my feelings during that time, the mandate to go to public high school seemed about as senseless and unfair to me as my mother's frequent attempts to alter my regular radio listening habits by constantly changing the station from one that was heavy on the Beatles to one that was exclusively rhythm and blues. As far as I was concerned, I had no identity crisis. After all, I knew who Martin Luther King was, I had been to the Apollo theater in Harlem several times, and I realized that my hair would never be as straight as Patty Duke's—at least not without a hot comb.

There is no doubt in my mind that my parents made the best decision. When I arrived in high school, I did have a little more than a passing knowledge of Latin and a familiarity with Spanish; to this day I can recite all prepositions within 30 seconds. On the other hand, there was not much emphasis on science and mathematics in my Catholic elementary school experience, and I remember the shock and embarrassment at what I did not know in my first public school science class—wasn't H_2O a cleaning fluid? The difference between *absolute wrong,* considered a mortal sin that sends one directly to hell without absolution, and *a little bit wrong,* considered a venial sin that can be absolved with sincere repentance prior to death, was an important distinction for me to recognize as a teenager.

Although, I was still chided a bit for being a "Catholic schoolgirl," going to a public high school that was approximately one-third African American was an excellent transition to prepare me for ultimately attending a historically Black university in the late 1960s and early 1970s. The fact that I subsequently attended a Catholic university for graduate school was sheer coincidence. However, my sense is that my Catholic elementary school experience served me well in negotiating the temperaments of the faculty and administrators who, from time to time, exhibited a "missionary" attitude toward students from third world cultures. I still maintain some strange habits that I am sure are lifetime endowments. For instance, in an environmentally incorrect manner, I still waste reams of paper by throwing them away if they have crossouts or erasure marks. I shy away from gospel music, in non-Catholic as well as Catholic settings, since I know that it shows disrespect to snap your fingers or dance to it, even though the beat and tempo of much of it is extremely similar to party music. Last, but certainly not least, you will always find me on the Virgin Mary's side of the church, for I still have the fear of God and feel more comfortable talking through her.

The notion that African American parents select Roman Catholic schools primarily for their academic successes is consistent in the literature (Polite, 1992) and in my personal experience. Clearly, my siblings and I were advantaged in many ways by attending an integrated, fairly well-endowed parochial school. We did get a good basic education, learned how to communicate in more than one culture, and do not consider white people as much of a mystery as do many of our friends and colleagues. The research also suggests that African American students fit neatly into the social sphere of integrated Catholic schools. Bauch (1988) states that "they are involved at least as well, if not better than non-Blacks" (p. 137), and Comer, Haynes, and Hamilton-Lee suggest that Catholic schools typically foster a "social integration" that is sensitive to the needs of African American children. Citing the work of Coleman and Hoffer, he notes that "this social integration stems from the human and social capital fostered by Catholic schools. Human capital is the development of skills and capabilities in individuals. Social capital is the relationship that exists among individuals" (p. 199).

Bauch (1988) notes in "Black Family Participation in Catholic Secondary Education" that there is a congruence, or "fit," between what parents want and what the school provides by way of academic and social development. I would argue that it is not a perfect fit by any measure—that parents, parents of color particularly, are frequently forced to tailor culturally their children's social development in Catholic schools regardless of the school's socioeconomic composition. While there is no doubt about the value of social integration, my experience suggests that African American parents feel comfortable in their ability to guide this dimension of their children's growth and development. It seems that they do not rely on, or possibly trust, Catholic school personnel to teach what they know and understand to be important about being African American in this nation. This being the case, educators in parochial schools should be challenged to find ways to engage parents in a greater way in the content, design, and delivery of instruction to African American students.

Catholic schools allowed me to prosper academically most likely because I was made to feel very much a part of a caring community, subject to this social integration, as Comer describes. The fact that this comfort zone allowed me to disregard the racial and ethnic differences between me and my classmates and presume that there was a similar environment in the world at large would have made me highly vulnerable and less successful later in life. It is likely for this reason that my parents, similar to Audre Lorde's parents in her autobiographical essay on her Catholic school experience (1992), chose to shield me from the harsh realities of life and racism for as long as they could through education in a caring community and then were compelled at a certain point to force me into a reality that they knew was there all along but were now confident that I had the academic, moral, and ethical background to negotiate.

REFERENCES

Bauch, P. A. (1988). Black family participation in Catholic secondary education. In D. T. Slaughter & D. J. Johnson (Eds.), *Visible now: Blacks in private schools* (pp. 122–142). Westport, CT: Greenwood.

Comer, J. P., Haynes, N. M., & Hamilton-Lee, M. (1987–1988) School power: A model for improving Black student achievement. *Urban League Review, 11*, 187–200.

Lorde, A. (1992). Zami: A new spelling of my name. In A. C. Sumrall & P. Vecchione (Eds.), *Catholic girls* (pp. 45–54). New York: Penguin.

Polite, V. (1992). Getting the job done well: African American students and Catholic schools. *Journal of Negro Education, 61*(2), 211–222.

CHAPTER 8

Act Your Age, Not Your Color

Lisa D. Delpit

On December 26, 1973, I attended the 75th anniversary celebration of St. Francis Xavier (SFX) Catholic Church in Baton Rouge, Louisiana. That year was also the 73rd anniversary of St. Francis Xavier School, which I attended from 1959 through 1965. Four generations of our family were represented at that anniversary celebration, and four generations of our family attended St. Francis—my 79-year-old mother, my older siblings, seven of my nine nieces and nephews, and the daughter of one nephew and the son of another. If I were a resident of Baton Rouge, my daughter would probably attend school there and I would likely be intimately involved with assisting the school in its development. There were many families present at the anniversary celebration whose strong familial connection to SFX resembled my own.

Why has this small, all–African American school continued to exist throughout its rocky history, and why is community loyalty so great? In order to suggest some answers to the questions of the school's longevity, I'd like to sketch the history of the school and share some of my own experiences there—both positive and negative.

HISTORY OF ST. FRANCIS XAVIER

When the first Catholic church in Baton Rouge, St. Joseph's, opened its doors in 1792, African American Catholics, both enslaved and free, were among its congregation. The Spanish and French priests of Louisiana parishes insisted that plantation owners baptize the people they had enslaved, and the priests held services both in the parish church and on the plantations on a regular basis. For more than 100 years African American Catholics worshiped in the back pews of St. Joseph's. After the Emancipation Proclamation, most walked more than two miles each way from the "colored settlement" each Sunday. It was said that the Catholic church always had an open-door policy: The color of your skin dictated how close you sat to it!

The aftermath of the Civil War in the late 1800s brought a population explosion of both blacks and whites, and the racial unrest of the early 1900s brought demands from the white population for racial separation. In 1911 the rector of St. Joseph's wrote to the archbishop in New Orleans to request that a church be built for the "colored population." While awaiting that decision, a new church, St. Agnes, built closer to the colored settlement, temporarily served a racially mixed congregation—most white parishioners sat on one side of the church, and Blacks and Italians sat on the other.

Amidst louder demands for separation from the predominantly white parishes, a new colored parish was approved in 1916 and parishioners began working on the new church building. For two years they planned and raised funds. According to a program distributed at the 75th anniversary celebration describing that period, "Stories abound of long days, from sunrise to dark, going up and down the river in buggies begging for food and donations to support the dinners and bazaars of the church."

The construction of the church—accomplished through the volunteer labor of skilled craftsmen in the congregation—was a labor of love. The doors opened in 1918 under the charge of the Josephite Fathers. In 1920, the same commitment brought the building of a new elementary school to be run by the Sisters of the Holy Family, an order of African American nuns. By 1943 the congregation numbered 2,000 and the school housed 600 students. In 1956, the parish dedicated the long-awaited high school.

By 1962 there were more than 3,000 African Americans on the church rolls, and the elementary and high school classrooms were overflowing. However, only six classes graduated from the beautiful new high school before tragedy struck. The federal government proposed to run an interstate highway directly through the African American community of Baton Rouge, thus separating relatives and neighbors and destroying the homes of hundreds of families. The new high school was directly in its path. Two nearby white parishes were also in the originally planned path of I-10 but were saved through who knows what kinds of deals and backdoor politicking. St. Francis Xavier was not so fortunate. Despite visits to Washington by prominent parishioners to plead their case, the new high school was demolished. Sadly, the building of I-10 also eventually necessitated the demolition of the church building because the pile drivers and heavy machinery used for the highway construction badly damaged the old structure, and there was no money for repairs.

For a while in the 1970s mass was offered in parishioners' homes until, by some miracle, the parish was able to raise $161,000, and the bishop approved a new church. There had been some doubt as to whether the church would receive approval from the bishop. Nearby St. Agnes had lost a number of members and was finding it difficult to maintain its parish. A committee of parishioners from St. Agnes petitioned the bishop *not* to build a new SFX but to merge the two parishes. As the pastor of St. Francis suggested in an interview, the white parishioners were attempting to save *their* parish by the merger. Ironically, white Catholics were now suffering the consequences of their earlier desire to distance themselves from their darker brethren. Despite all efforts to the contrary, the new St. Francis Xavier Church was dedicated in September 1978.

The strategy of promoting inclusion to secure self-preservation had been practiced with greater success earlier in Baton Rouge's white Catholic history. In the late 1960s St. Agnes school had begun losing enrollment. The archdiocese created an interparochial system in which students from St. Francis Xavier or St. Agnes parish would attend the school closer to their home. This boosted enrollments at St. Agnes but created a drastic decline in enrollment at St. Francis, putting the school at risk of closing. The parishioners rallied once more, holding prayer vigils and other peaceful protests to rectify the situation. The school was saved, and by 1993 and the anniversary celebration, the school was once more filled to capacity.

MY HISTORY AT ST. FRANCIS XAVIER

Although my parents wanted me to attend St. Francis Xavier, my preschool teacher recommended that I begin first grade at age 5; the Catholic schools would only allow 6-year-olds into first grade. Therefore, I began in public school and transferred to the Catholic school in third grade in 1959.

I think all of us who are of similar age and who went to Catholic schools share some distinct memories. For example, most Americans probably believe that the Cuban missile crisis was averted for political or power reasons. We who were in Catholic schools in the 1960s, however, know that we prayed it over. As with various other of our country's crises during the 1960s, the Catholic children of America, putting their studies aside for the good of the nation, spent days in church and said rosary after rosary to save the world.

This was the time of much national madness. Children were drilled in what to do in the event of nuclear attack (get under your desk and put your hands over your head). Sirens would sound periodically so parents could practice picking their children up quickly in case the Russians attacked. Everyone had to learn what food should be stored in an underground bomb shelter (never mind that, due to the high water level, no one in Louisiana had a basement, much less a bomb shelter!). The only difference, I suppose, for those in Catholic schools was that formal, collective prayers were always a part of our drills.

I also remember other kinds of frenzy that developed among my schoolmates that might have been a bit different from others' Catholic school experiences. During the politically heady 1960s, a rumor would periodically spread through the student body that the Ku Klux Klan was on its way to the school to attack us. I don't know if the adults ever knew what was being whispered on the playground from one wide-eyed youngster to another, but the fear attached to the rumor was not without grounding, since all African Americans in Louisiana at that time knew of and were fearful of the KKK. In that regard, the school—not through its official curriculum, but through its informal grapevine—was definitely a reflection of the community it served.

There was a certain seamlessness between home and school for most of the students (although not for all, as I'll discuss). Like the parents of many other students, my own parents, particularly my father, were deeply involved with the church. The school and church were a significant part of the community's social life: the twice-yearly bazaars, the weekly bingo games, the school performances, the adult dances, even the weddings, baptisms, funerals, and wakes.

The church was not the only meeting place for parents and school personnel, both lay and religious; parents, principals, and teachers all interacted in everyday life in the larger African American community. Because of the housing realities in the segregated South, most African Americans lived in close proximity to one another. Many lay teachers and nuns were related to the students; at the very least, the teachers or their own parents probably knew or socialized with the parents or grandparents of some of the students. Attitudes, notions of discipline, and notions of what constituted excellent instruction were shared between school and home.

The instruction was essentially Eurocentric. The only reference I recall to Africa was collecting money to send to the missionaries to save the souls of the poor pagan children there. The materials were limited.

We usually got the textbooks after the white public schools and then the white Catholic schools were done with them. Needless to say, they were not only completely Eurocentric but also dismally outdated. Instruction was limited in scope but rigorous in form. Less content was taught, but what was taught was expected to be learned—and it was.

There was no assumption that being Black meant you couldn't learn—if that were the case, then our teachers wouldn't have learned because they were all Black. In fact, the message was instead that we had to be smarter than white kids if we were going to be able to be anything. The other message was not that we *could* learn, but that we *would* learn. Corporal punishment was prevalent—not only for disciplinary purposes, but for failure to master content as well. I recall pinches for misnaming the parts of speech and ruler hits for not forming a cursive capital *A* correctly.

Instruction was very didactic. There was little, if any, student-initiated writing. Yet I attribute my comfort with "edited" English and my ability to write with confidence now to the daily sentence diagraming drills those teachers led with unmitigated exuberance.

Perhaps this diligent attention to standard forms was particularly appropriate for the "Black English–speaking" population the school served. The careful attention to language structure focused our awareness on the differences between our spoken language and written edited English in ways that discussions or mere corrections could not.

Although Black English usage was corrected with a vengeance, I can recall the teachers occasionally uttering some version of Black—or Creole—English construction. Indeed, the teachers themselves were bidialectical and actually provided unintentional role models for appropriate code-switching between Black and standard English.

Questioning of content was not encouraged—or even permitted—in the classroom. But even with the very teacher-centered instruction and focus on adult-administered discipline, there was a great deal of responsibility given over to children. Those students who were more capable were often put in charge of tutoring less capable classmates. Substitute teachers were seldom needed. As a fourth grader who was doing well in school, I was often asked to "take over" for a temporarily absent teacher. I was not the only older student encouraged to be responsible for peers and younger students. It was a community value that easily transferred to school life.

As I think back on the attitudes of those teachers, I realize that they never equated ignorance with a lack of intelligence. They knew that some of their students would not know math or standard English or how to read. Yet they assumed their students had the academic sense to learn anything they were taught—if they were taught correctly—and the common sense to take on what some might assume to be adult responsibilities. There was no question in these teachers' minds that they were working with competent human beings.

All of my experiences at SFX were not positive. The close connection with the community had some inherent drawbacks. The school, like most schools, was a conservative institution that tended to reflect the most conservative elements of the community it served. Working-class and middle-class southern Black communities of the early 1960s carried a lot of burdens. Perhaps their heaviest burden was to *prove* that they were acceptable to the white world, that morally the civil rights movement was right to demand a society not separated by race. Their proof often entailed finding ways to distance themselves from the unenlightened Black masses, whose behaviors they considered unacceptable to the white world.

Although Catholic schools are known for a certain amount of sexual repressiveness, I believe these Black Catholic teachers took sexual repressiveness to a new level. Clearly, any hint of sexuality had to be snuffed out if we were to dispel the white myth of Black sexual licentiousness. One of my sixth-grade classmates was severely punished because one of the Sisters "heard" that she allowed a boy to walk her home. Prior to a seventh-grade dance, another Sister took a yardstick and made some very reluctant boys and girls practice dancing with the yardstick stretched between them to inform us of the proper distance to be maintained between dancing partners. I later realized that this was not the norm for Catholic schools, when, after transferring to a newly integrated white Catholic high school, I discovered, to my surprise, that the white nuns readily entered into conversations with the girls about their boyfriends and relationships.

The self-deprecating machinations of the Black Catholic nuns were psychically damaging in other ways, too. I recall what we were told whenever someone misbehaved. Particularly when we were the only Black children at some diocese event, we were admonished vehemently to "act your age, not your color."

I remember an occasion when the white bishop was making a visit to a school program commemorating a big anniversary of St. Francis Xavier Church. The school choir had been practicing for weeks for the event. The Sister leading the choir had chosen as one of our songs "Sleep Kentucky Babe," after hearing that the bishop liked Stephen Foster's songs. Several days before the big event, we performed for the principal and the teachers. Afterwards there was a flurry of disapproval. The problem turned out to be that the second verse contained a line, "Possum fo' you breakfast when your sleeping time is done." Now that just sounded too "colored." After meetings of the faculty, the teachers spent hours making sure that we knew the revised version—"Cereal for your breakfast . . ." — which was deemed sufficiently mainstream to present to the bishop.

This attempt to "whitewash" ourselves had more sinister repercussions. Because of the history of the French and Spanish in Louisiana, Creole families—families of African, French, Spanish, and Indian ancestry—varied greatly in skin tone and hair texture. Many of my "Black" classmates were very light-skinned with straight blond hair and/or blue eyes. So European-featured were some of these children that I—fair, freckled, and red-headed—was not considered particularly light-skinned, especially since I had "nappy" hair.

In a recent book chronicling the lives of African American women, Sara Lawrence Lightfoot (1994) recounts the story of a former nun now in her 50s. "Toni," in discussing her life in the Catholic Church, returns again to comparisons of her own brown skin to the lighter skin of, first, her schoolmates, and, later, many of her fellow nuns. In discussing the effect of the omnipresent color stratification in her own life during the 1950s and 1960s, Toni "admits that even her 'middle' darkness might have prohibited her from gaining access to certain educational opportunities if she had not been such a stunningly successful student: '*I* got the opportunity because I was so bright they couldn't deny it'" (pp. 251–252). Yet Toni thought herself less beautiful than her lighter-skinned comrades. Lightfoot comments: "Like so many black women of her generation, she had inherited the damaging legacy of measuring her beauty by the texture of her hair and the color of her skin" (p. 228).

This self-undermining legacy has roots that run strong and deep. As soon as the larger society attempted to justify the enslavement of a darker people by refuting their humanity, belittling their intelligence, and castigating their beauty, self-doubt began to take hold in the African American consciousness. Giving undue homage to "whiteness" has been well documented in writings as early as 1904, when African American activist Fannie H. Burroughs criticized Black men who would choose a wife on the basis of her light skin "color rather than her character" (cited in Giddings, 1984). Historian and African American feminist Paula Giddings (1984) reports that even during great surges of racial pride among the African American community, such as the Marcus Garvey movement in post–World War I America, white-as-ideal remained embedded in the larger African American psyche—so much so that the *New York Times* questioned the sincerity of the Garvey movement by noting the prevalence of hair straighteners and skin lighteners such as "Black-No-More" in the African American community.

This focus on "white-as-ideal" at St. Francis Xavier led to a real and painful caste system. Darker-skinned children were not supported in quite the same way as lighter-skinned students. Although all students were expected to learn, lighter-skinned students were expected to learn more. Lighter-skinned students who were clearly less academically gifted were led to believe that they were bright, while brilliant darker-skinned children were never given the public praise they deserved.

I was somewhat of an outsider, for I entered the school late and was not from one of the leading Creole families. Thus I think I was able to see the caste system more clearly than some of the other lighter-skinned students. Still, I was not fully aware of what had been happening until I was an adult and talked to some of my darker-skinned former schoolmates. The pain that this system caused was undeniable and inexcusable. I must add that these attitudes were not found only in the school. The school merely reflected the pathological reactions to white supremacy prevalent in much of the African American community at large.

Still, most of my classmates—of whatever complexion—who continued in school did well. After eighth grade I transferred to a newly integrated Catholic school in a white parish. I remember being shocked to discover that I and most of my classmates from SFX excelled. In fact, even though there was much overt racism, many of the year-end awards in particular subject areas went to Black students. In fact, the Black students did so well that, two years after integration, the white parish decided to close the school. The parish could not reconcile itself to supporting a school in which "those niggers" were cheating their children out of the academic honors that were their just due.

No matter which high school SFX students subsequently attended, they represented themselves well. Although I don't have exact numbers, almost all of the classmates I can recall attended college. One young man who didn't, I remember tutoring when we were in the fifth grade. He had a difficult time learning to read and write and would probably be diagnosed as dyslexic were he in today's schools. Although he was not considered college material, he is now one of the biggest property owners and most successful businessmen in the city. In part, I attribute that to the assumption with which we were all continually bombarded—that no matter what, we would do well. Despite his difficulty with school tasks, he was never led to believe that he was incapable of functioning in the real out-of-school world.

CONCLUSION

I have often asked myself what has caused St. Francis Xavier to have survived so long. Today the school is thriving, although there are only a few nuns and the school is staffed primarily with lay teachers, many of whom attended SFX as youngsters. One of the factors that is maintained is a cultural connection to the community and a belief that the students will learn.

I recently talked to a woman who taught first grade when I was in school. She taught for 45 years, retired, and is now back "helping out" the first-grade teacher. I asked her what was different about herself and the teachers at the public schools now. Mrs. Hebert told me that what was different was how she determined who was at fault when the children failed to learn. She told me about her high school chemistry teacher, who was a model for her own teaching. When the entire class failed a test, the teacher closed the book and started over again. She said that when over half the class failed to learn something, it wasn't the children, it was the teacher. Mrs. Hebert never forgot that. She was taught the same lesson in the Black teachers college she attended and had the idea reinforced when she student-taught with the Black nuns in New Orleans.

I can see the difference in my nieces and nephews who attended SFX for only a few years and then transferred to more conveniently located, predominantly white schools when they moved to another part of the city. Whereas I had always been taught that we should be *smarter* than white kids, somehow these children learned in predominantly white settings that they would be doing well if they did *almost* as good as white kids. I still remember complaining to one of my nephews about a D on his eighth-grade report card. His response, "Gosh, what do you want, the white kids get Cs!" I was dumbfounded.

Despite my work now to get more African and African American material into all schools' curricula, I am struck with my own history. Although there was no Afrocentric curriculum in my elementary school, St. Francis Xavier, what was there was a belief in African American people.

The children who attended St. Francis were a part of a larger extended family, a family that had to collectively do battle to survive. The teachers and parents battled racism together, sharing not only their identity as African Americans but a sense that their common destiny depended on the success of the children in the school.

The African American parishioners had a history of working together toward a goal and of accomplishing wonders with little resources. Can there be any doubt that the teachers' attitudes toward the children as potentially competent learners stemmed in large part from their knowledge of the lives of the children's parents and grandparents? Many of these parents and grandparents were not themselves formally schooled (my own father only completed eighth grade), yet they built three church buildings and three school buildings from the ground up. They organized protests to the archdiocese as well as to the federal government. The teachers knew these children could perform, and they insisted on it. The seamlessness of the school–home experience for most of the children, as well as the high expectations and the academic discipline, converged to provide the kind of education that allowed students to enter into the mainstream and perform.

Most of my former classmates with whom I am still in contact have rejected the color and caste distinctions promoted by SFX. In fact, we all chuckle at the "browning" of the Creole line. Almost all the very light-skinned individuals have beautiful brown children. What they haven't rejected, and still remember with appreciation, is the sound academic background they received. But even more, they appreciate that our teachers held high expectations that we could—and *would*—learn.

REFERENCES

Giddings, P. (1984). *When and where I enter: The impact of Black women on race and sex in America.* New York: Bantam.

Lightfoot, S. L. (1994). *I've known rivers: Lives of loss and liberation.* Reading, MA: Addison-Wesley.

CHAPTER 9

Growing Up Black and Catholic in Louisiana: Personal Reflections on Catholic Education

Antoine M. Garibaldi

As I have progressed through my career over the past 20 years, I continually reflect on the excellent academic preparation that I received in my elementary and secondary schools. That education was provided by a group of Black nuns and a religious order of mostly white priests who expected me and my peers to succeed one day in a society that was more integrated and less discriminatory than the one in which we were growing up. These two religious orders, the Sisters of the Holy Family and the Josephite Fathers, have made tremendous contributions in African American communities throughout the South; and, were it not for their establishment of schools in Louisiana, many Blacks would not have had the opportunity to obtain an education because of the few public schools Blacks could attend prior to the 1960s.

This chapter of personal reflections, therefore, is devoted to the Catholic educational experiences that I received from the Sisters of the Holy Family and the Josephite Fathers in New Orleans between 1956 and 1964, and from eight and a half years in the Josephites' minor and major seminaries in Newburgh, New York, and Washington, D.C., respectively. As you will see, the elementary and secondary experiences in New Orleans, which were in all-Black settings, were distinctively different from the more racially integrated Catholic school experiences of some of the other authors in this book. In addition to receiving an education, I felt that I was getting a daily lesson in civics because the purposeful commitment and dedication to bring about equality of educational opportunity in a segregated southern community and in a racially separate Catholic

Church was a major goal of the two religious congregations that shaped my future.

Though much of the following recollection is intended to be personal interpretations of my Catholic education, the discussion can also be seen in a contemporary theoretical context of concern with successful educational environments. Schools like St. Joan of Arc and St. Augustine were successful because they had the five critical elements that Brookover has defined as characteristics of "effective schools": (1) Teachers believed that all children could learn, and they set high expectations and standards of achievement; (2) a safe, orderly, and work-oriented learning environment existed; (3) the principal was the instructional leader who promoted effective instruction and high achievement for all students; (4) parents were actively involved in the school program; and (5) academic progress was constantly monitored and regular feedback was provided to students (Brookover, 1985; Brookover, Beady, Flood, Schweitzer, and Wisenbaker, 1979; Brookover & Lezotte, 1979). Even though Brookover colleagues' research came many years after the establishment of these schools in the South, the five essential factors of "effective schools" will be easily discernible in the following discussion.

HISTORICAL BACKGROUND

Unlike the situation in many other states in this country, Catholic schools were plentiful in Louisiana throughout much of the late 1800s and in the 1900s. One of the primary reasons for their existence was the early settlement of the French and Spanish, who brought their Catholic religious traditions with them to this region. Thus schools were established by Catholic missionaries to augment those few that already existed and also to serve as a vehicle for evangelization. Among this group were elementary and secondary Catholic schools established to serve African American students because "separate but equal" laws in Louisiana's cities and towns, which are still called parishes, prohibited Blacks from attending schools with whites. Religious congregations that dedicated themselves to nonwhite populations therefore viewed Louisiana and nearby states as fertile areas to establish schools because of the large number of Black Catholics there and the limited educational opportunities available to Blacks due to the strict enforcement of segregation and Jim Crow laws.

One of Louisiana's oldest Catholic congregations serving African Americans was a religious order of Black nuns, the Sisters of the Holy Family. Founded officially in 1842 by a free woman of color, Henriette

Delille, along with Juliette Gaudin and Josephine Charles, this small group of nuns, with the assistance of laypersons, served the sick, the poor, the enslaved, and the orphaned in New Orleans. During her brief 50 years of life, Mother Delille and her followers established schools for the poor, night schools for slaves after the Civil War, and a school for "free colored girls from families of means" (Detiege, 1976). After her death in 1862, St. Mary's Academy, the first secondary school established for African American girls, and which remains today an excellent high school, was founded in 1867. The Sisters of the Holy Family established several schools in New Orleans and in other parts of the state, and they were the first teachers of my siblings and me from the early 1940s to the 1960s at St. Joan of Arc School. St. Joan of Arc was coincidentally the first church established in New Orleans by the Society of St. Joseph of the Sacred Heart, the Josephite Fathers, in 1909. The Josephite Fathers and Brothers, a predominantly white order of priests and brothers, came to this country from England to serve Black Catholics. They established parishes, built churches, and eventually constructed schools for the numerous southern communities they served. The Josephites, the Sisters of the Holy Family, and the Sisters of the Blessed Sacrament—whose foundress, Blessed Katharine Drexel, founded Xavier University in 1915—have had a profound impact on the lives of many Blacks—Catholic and non-Catholic—in the South, as well as in other parts of the country. My brief recollections of my days at St. Joan of Arc Elementary School and St. Augustine's High School are snapshots of very rich, comprehensive educational experiences, and it is important that we reflect on their measures of success and document them for their historical and educational value.

ST. JOAN OF ARC SCHOOL

Until the early 1960s, all Catholic schools and churches were segregated in New Orleans. I walked about eight blocks to St. Joan of Arc every day with my older and younger brothers and sisters, but many of my classmates who walked to school passed as many as five all-white Catholic schools on their way. Some even came from as far as five miles away on one of our parish's school buses. We could only attend St. Joan of Arc because it was the only all-Black Catholic school in our area of the city. I was certainly old enough to question how this segregation could exist in the Catholic Church, where all were supposed to be recognized as children of the same God, but I found it hard to understand and believe this given the religious principles and doctrines we were learning. Even more, I used to wonder how older Black Catholics had been able to maintain their faith despite this obvious system of inequality. My classmates and I accepted the racial dichotomy that existed in our community as well, but we also realized and were taught that we could change this societal circumstance with hard work and effort. Thus the nuns believed and demonstrated to us that we could all learn; they motivated us to do well academically; and they constantly reminded us that we were as good as our racially different counterparts, many of whom shared our religious affiliation.

Financial and Parental Support

St. Joan of Arc was one of several all-Black grammar (K–8) schools in the city. As was the case in many other similar schools, St. Joan of Arc parents believed in the quality of the education that the Sisters of the Holy Family provided, and they made significant financial sacrifices for this special educational opportunity. Though per-student tuition costs of less than $1 monthly in the 1950s might not seem high in 1996 dollars (it was 60¢ monthly in the 1950s, before increasing to $1.25), the "price" of our elementary education was very substantial for most of the working-class families whose children attended all-Black Catholic schools in New Orleans. Discounts in the form of graduated tuition fees were given to families, like mine, with more than one child in attendance (my parents usually had four of their nine children in school at any given time), but every family was expected to make other contributions by supporting and/or organizing small fundraisers at school and in their neighborhoods. For example, during recess and after school, students would sell single pieces of candy (usually fudge at a nickel a piece), small bags of popcorn, candied apples, and other food items that had been prepared by their families. The proceeds were given to the school, and each student had a similar opportunity during the year as part of his or her class's fundraising effort. The nuns themselves also purchased and made food items (e.g., potato chips, "handsuckers," candy, frozen cups) to sell. Several families held school-sponsored suppers at their homes, and students' families were expected to support these activities throughout the school year. Additional support came from the weekly collections of the church parish, school raffles, and church fundraisers such as the annual bazaar. With limited funds to operate, every contribution was extremely important to the support of the school's educational program and the maintenance of a very old physical plant. Thus all parents and students recognizedthat they had critical roles to play in helping to support the school financially, and they were expected to be active participants and volunteers in the school's activities, regardless of their religious affiliation. My eight brothers and sisters and I learned early that the "price" of our education did not cover the real "costs" of the education we were receiving.

The strong bond that existed between home and school was a critical factor in the success of schools like St. Joan of Arc. Black parents who made the financial sacrifice to send their children to Catholic schools did so because of the excellent quality of education and because of the order and discipline to which their children were exposed and which they were taught. Report card conferences, PTA meetings, and school activities were mandatory, and parents accepted responsibility for those instances when their children did not do what was expected of them. In other words, parents "bought into" the school program and contributed to the school's success by helping out when there was a need for their assistance.

Quality of Instruction and School Climate

The Sisters of the Holy Family taught almost every grade at St. Joan of Arc during my elementary school years. (There were probably three lay teachers during my time there, and they had been carefully selected by the principal and the rest of the faculty.) The Sisters were excellent and challenging teachers, and it was not until some years later that I realized that some of the nuns who were teaching were simultaneously working on their college degrees at Xavier University. They demanded and expected orderly classrooms, enforced discipline, and motivated students to do their very best—constantly reminding us that getting an education was a serious matter in a society that offered few occupations for Blacks to pursue. The Sisters also inculcated and reinforced the importance of values such as honesty, integrity, and service, and they helped each one of us to develop strong self-concepts and self-esteem. More than any other goal, they expected all students to achieve to their potential and to be successful in their adult years.

Non-Catholics were a significant segment of the student population, but they were rarely singled out because of their religious affiliation. They were required, however, to attend school masses and religious celebrations of the church. Non-Catholic parents were more concerned about their children obtaining a good education and less worried that their child would be converted to Catholicism.

Even without the newest educational resources, the Sisters of the Holy Family and the few lay teachers at St. Joan of Arc did their best with the teaching materials available to them. Thus "used" textbooks were staples in most classes. But I never felt that I was receiving anything less than an outstanding education. The teachers taught all students as if they could learn, and excuses for unsatisfactory academic performance were unacceptable. Pride in each individual's past and ability, as well as acceptance of the task to achieve, were all key features of St. Joan of Arc's effective educational program, and the success of many of the school's alumni has confirmed what teachers and parents already knew.

Because there were limited social and cultural opportunities for Blacks in rigidly segregated New Orleans, St. Joan of Arc was also the center of social and cultural activities. School plays and dances, picnics, teas and banquets, festivals, athletic events, field trips, and more were organized by the school, and they were used as a vehicle to bring families and students closer together. One memorable event was a school field trip to see the movie *Ben Hur* at one of the white movie theaters. Since there were only two Black theaters in the city, the chance to see a movie at a private screening matinee and at a place where Blacks were usually not legally allowed was a special event for all of us. Those barriers of segregation were eventually eliminated after organized boycotts and pickets throughout the city and with the passage of the Civil Rights Act of 1964, but the early exposure we were given to societal, educational, employment, and economic inequities, as well as social injustice, served as ample motivation to become more active in the struggle for equal rights. St. Joan of Arc gave its graduates the necessary foundation to both succeed in high school and to change the course of history through service and civic involvement.

ST. AUGUSTINE HIGH SCHOOL

In 1963 I left my classmates of the last seven years at St. Joan of Arc and was accepted to attend the eighth grade at the all-Black, all-male St. Augustine's High School, founded in 1951 by the Josephite Fathers. It was a decision that brought mixed emotions for me; on the one hand, I would be attending the outstanding school from which my three older brothers had graduated, but I would not have an eighth-grade graduation at St. Joan of Arc. I was, however, excited at the opportunity, especially since I was planning to leave New Orleans and enter the seminary in ninth grade. Students admitted to the eighth grade had to perform well on a standardized test given to many applicants. And since I was not a good standardized test taker, I knew that I was selected because of my interest in becoming a Josephite priest and my good grades at St. Joan of Arc. Although I was uncertain of my ability to achieve and compete in this new academic environment, once there I rose to the demands of the mostly white faculty of priests and some lay Black men in the same way I did, and was taught, at St. Joan of Arc. We were taught that we were as good as anyone else, and we accepted that challenge with the vigor and zeal of a fierce competitor. Even though we could not compete at academic and athletic rallies with any of the predominantly white schools in those days, it was not long before we would have the chance to demonstrate how well prepared we were.

Instructional Quality and School Climate

St. Augustine's High School quickly became a recognized educational institution in the city during the 1950s. Beginning with its first class of 138 young men and a faculty of six Josephites and one layman, the new school had limited science facilities, no auditorium, no gym, and a muddy field for recreation (Boucree & Garibaldi, 1989). But St. Augustine was a school where excellence was expected of all of its students despite the fact that the academic abilities of its student body varied from homeroom to homeroom. The school had a strong core curriculum in the sciences, mathematics, and the humanities, and writing and speaking skills were given special priority. (I especially remember our use of *Time* magazine as a tool for developing writing skills, as well as a vehicle for keeping up to date with current events, especially the impact that the civil rights movement was having on barriers of discrimination and the political climate of the nation.) St. Augustine's young men were addressed as "Mr." by their teachers (what a powerful way of conveying dignity and confidence to Black men in the 1950s and 1960s), and that individual respect set the tone for the exacting standards that all of us were expected to meet. "St. Aug. men" were also taught that they were more than just students at this school; they were also expected to exemplify the values and principles of the school by the way they carried themselves in their neighborhoods and in the New Orleans community.

For the first dozen years of its existence, St. Augustine easily recruited the very best and most talented African American young men to its school; but when parochial schools began to integrate during the mid-1960s, other formerly all-white Catholic secondary schools gradually began to recruit some of the young Black men who might have gone to St. Aug. Nevertheless, St. Aug. tried to bring down other barriers when it filed a suit against the Louisiana High School Athletic Association (LHSAA) in 1967 in federal court. The precedent-setting legal decision not only gained St. Augustine's admittance into the league, but it also ended all racially separate athletic leagues in the city and the state. Track meets, American Legion baseball, and the city's recreation department programs were no longer separated. And, in keeping with its goal of making it possible for all its students to compete with students from other schools, science fairs and other academic competitions were no longer segregated. St. Augustine's students were ready for the challenge, and they performed well in city and state academic rallies.

Discipline was very strict at St. Augustine's, and each of us was taught that discipline was a means to a greater end, namely, a requirement for success in a competitive and challenging world where dreams could be fulfilled despite the lingering vestiges of segregation and discrimination in all walks of life. All of us knew that the usual and dreaded consequence of "behavior unbecoming a St. Aug. man" was a few swats of the paddle, but that "board of education" was a form of corporal punishment to be avoided and a reminder of the discipline that was expected. Immediate expulsion for unruly behavior or serious academic failure was another possible consequence, and disciplinary policies were taken seriously by students, teachers, and administrators.

Financial and Parental Support

It was an honor and a privilege to attend St. Augustine, but many who wanted to go could not do so because of the cost. Tuition was $7 a month in the mid 1950s ($12 monthly in 1963–64, when I was in the eighth grade), but many young men whose families could not afford the tuition were given the opportunity to work around the school after class hours and over the weekend, doing odd jobs such as cutting the grass, working in the lunchroom, or cleaning the building in exchange for their tuition and daily lunch. My three older brothers, who attended St. Augustine's at the same time in the late 1950s, were able to combine this in-kind support for working after school with the money they earned from their weekend jobs as caddies at the all-white golf park to cover the cost of their tuition, bus fare, and meals. The Josephites underwrote those in-kind "scholarships," and many young men received an education because of that special opportunity.

The continuation of St. Augustine's High School, like many other religious-affiliated schools, has not come about because of a large endowment or substantial support from the Catholic Church. Tuition supports only about 60% of the school's educational and general expenditures, and the remainder comes from contributions of the Josephite Fathers, parent fundraisers, the alumni, and the community. Financial support of more than $1 million, a sum that does not include an annual $200,000 of contributed services from the priests' salaries, has been provided by the Josephites through the school's first four decades. The Josephites receive no compensation for their work and return their salaries to the school's operating fund. But because of the smaller number of religious who teach at the school, much more money has been needed to pay the salaries of lay teachers. The dedication of these individuals, more than half of whom are alumni and several of whom have taught there since the 1950s, has been crucial to the preservation of the principles and traditions of the school. And, as was the case at St. Joan of Arc, fundraising by students and parents continues to be essential to maintaining a school with fewer students than in years past.

Societal demands for more educational opportunities for African American men make St. Augustine's mission more valuable today than when it was originally founded in 1951. The socioeconomic backgrounds of the students' families, for example, provide a revealing picture of St. Aug.'s population today: 25% come from low-income families, 55% of parents have a high school education, and 35% of the students come from one-parent homes. Thus St. Augustine continues to serve an important community and national need despite the school's limited resources. Such is the case of most Catholic educational institutions that have survived in urban and rural areas of the country, but that has rarely been an obstacle to the fulfillment of their mission.

Local and National Impact

St. Augustine's graduates have made a tremendous impact on the city of New Orleans, the state, and the nation. But even more important is the fact that at least half of St. Augustine's current faculty and administrators are graduates of their alma mater. Many of the city's and the state's leading African American politicians, including the former mayor of New Orleans, graduated from St. Augustine's. The more than 5,000 alumni include educators at all levels, including college presidents and school superintendents, accountants and bankers, physicians, businessmen, scientists, attorneys, musicians, artists and actors, television reporters and broadcast executives, athletes, numerous public officials, and many more. Six Presidential Scholars, more than the number from any other Catholic school in Louisiana, have been educated at St. Augustine's, and large numbers have gone on to some of the most selective colleges and universities in the country.

St. Augustine High School is also well known around the country for the outstanding accomplishments of its athletic teams, which have won state championships several times; its nationally recognized band, The Marching 100, is sought after for national parades and professional football games; and its success in academic competitions continues to win many of its students scholarships to colleges and universities throughout the nation.

Much credit is due to the Josephite Fathers and Brothers for the success of their graduates today because many of the priests in the 1950s and 1960s even risked their lives as they challenged a discriminatory and unfair system of segregation in New Orleans. Many whites in the community who were content with the status quo saw the Josephites as "troublemakers" and liberal men from the East Coast who had no business tampering with Jim Crow segregation. They were targeted by civic organizations such as the White Citizens Council, and many white Catholics vehemently disapproved of their legal challenges to athletic and academic activities for segregated schools. The priests' public positions on social policies were well known, and they were active in Black community organizations such as the Urban League and NAACP during the civil rights boycotts, protests, and demonstrations. Thus students at the high school were encouraged to get involved in many of the nonviolent movements that would eventually bring about voting rights, equal employment opportunities, and increased political participation for and by Blacks. My own interest in service to my community was reinforced by my one year at St. Augustine, and the experiences solidified my desire and plan to enter the seminary in ninth grade.

SEMINARY LIFE

When I left New Orleans to enter the Josephite minor seminary, Epiphany Apostolic College, in Newburgh, New York, in 1964, my decision to consider the religious life had been largely influenced by the work of the Josephites in my parish, at St. Augustine High School, and in other parishes in New Orleans and the South. Catholic school students were regularly visited by priests, brothers, and nuns who were recruiting for vocations, and many students filled out the cards and checked the affirmative boxes where it indicated "I would like to be a priest, brother, or nun." Most of us were too young to know what we truly wanted to become when we grew up, but it seemed that expressing interest in the religious life was the right thing to do at the time. However, most of us had never seen more than a few Black priests during our short lives. One of them was a St. Joan of Arc student who became a Josephite and who taught at St. Aug. Another was a recently ordained Society of the Divine Word priest who resided at the parish during the summer months while working on his master's degree at Loyola University. He was every young man's role model—smart, handsome, "hip" (as we used to say to indicate how "cool" someone was), and a "real people person" who was loved by all of the parishioners. But he was also a priest, and his "humanness" was both refreshing and magnetic. Thus I was very interested in making a commitment to work in the Black community as a priest, and the diverse ministry of the Josephites provided numerous possibilities.

Since I had also been an altar boy for several years at St. Joan of Arc, I was attracted to the ceremony of the Church as well. I had "performed" my share of masses at home—using grape juice and small flat circles of bread, sometimes even "Necco" candies, as my substitutes for wine and communion wafers, respectively—but that imitation of rituals and role models was consistent with behavior that would be exhibited by an adolescent interested in a particular career. I felt certain that I wanted to become a priest by the beginning of the seventh grade, but, as mentioned earlier, I also wanted to follow in the footsteps of my three older brothers, who had attended and graduated from St. Augustine's. Thus my eighth-grade year as a St. Aug. student became a brief opportunity for me to have that experience before entering the Josephite seminary in New York.

Entering a seminary more than a thousand miles away from home at 14 years of age was as difficult for me as it was for my parents, who, despite having eight other children, would have to adjust to my absence for nine months a year. None of my five older brothers and sisters had ever left home for an extended period by this time, so the decision to allow me to leave was not an easy one. Homesickness was not an easy adjustment for me initially either, but it helped to have others at the seminary who came from the same local area. (There were at least ten Black seminarians from the New Orleans area, and we rode the train together on those long rides to New York City in those early days, thereby significantly easing the worries of our parents.) The camaraderie of my peers and fellow New Orleanians, especially the upperclassmen, made the transition to this new life and place in upstate New York much easier.

Many of the more than 100 seminarians, many of whom were from New York, Pennsylvania, and the South, had begun their training as freshmen in high school at Epiphany, so my own situation of starting out young was not that unusual. Even more surprising, close to half of the Josephite seminarians were African American, a very rare situation compared to the many other seminaries that surrounded us in this area 60 miles north of New York City. At Epiphany there were six grade levels—high school freshman to college sophomore—but college students were not supposed to fraternize with the high school guys. That rule, however, was no longer enforced by 1967 because of a 50% reduction in our seminary enrollment. This was a time of major upheaval in the Church as Catholics reacted to the pronouncements of Pope John XXIII's Vatican Council II and as, at the same time, the civil rights protests against segregation in many cities influenced major changes in Catholic dioceses across the country. This declining seminary enrollment was also occurring at a time when many nuns, brothers, and priests were leaving their religious congregations as well. Thus the need for vocations was stronger than ever.

Growing up in the seminary was very much like attending a boarding school, with the exception of the hours we devoted to daily prayer and spiritual reflection. All attention was therefore focused on our vocation to become priests who would work in African American communities. Because we came from so many different cities and states, from varied ethnic and socioeconomic backgrounds, and from small and large families, we had the best of what society refers to today as "diversity." We learned about and from each other every day as we grew up as adolescents and young adults in a very insulated environment. As is natural in families of many siblings, we had our share of brotherly disagreements; but the anger was short-lived as we found ourselves within hours sitting next to each other in chapel or in the refectory for meals, walking in pairs saying the rosary outside, or getting ready for bed in the dormitory. It was a valuable experience for all of us, and one which has paid off in our adult lives. We learned to live together in a multiracial community while the rest of the country was debating the advantages and disadvantages of integration and equal opportunity for all. It was also good training for us as we contemplated the kinds of challenges we might one day face in our future southern parishes.

Education consumed a large part of our daily lives in the seminary, and the courses we took were of the highest quality. English and Latin were taught in every grade, and all of the other standard core courses (e.g., mathematics, history, and science) were a part of the curriculum. Our teachers, all but two of whom were priests and brothers, were very demanding, and we knew how critical it was to succeed in the classroom if we wanted to continue pursuing our vocation. (In fact, most of us dreaded those fateful days at the end of the school year when the faculty met in closed-door sessions to determine who would stay and who would not return. If you were called by the rector, you automatically knew what the decision was, and the sad task of bidding farewell to friends and classmates would begin.) Mandatory, proctored "study halls" of about one hour every night gave each student a chance to prepare for the next day's assignments, and many guys had their small flashlights so they could study surreptitiously under their sheets after lights went out in the dormitory after 9:30. Getting caught talking or studying after lights went out could mean "jug," the seminary's version of detention. Sanctions in "jug" included manual labor or temporary loss of recreation privileges. But you could also be "grounded," losing the opportunity to go for a walk off the property into town on a "free day" (usually Wednesday and Sunday). Nevertheless, the discipline was part of the formation process, and those who could not cope with the seminary's rules usually left before the school year ended. It took some only a few days at the seminary to decide that this highly ordered and regimented system was not the life for them, and those who did not live very far away would have their parents pick them up in a matter of hours.

Life in the novitiate—a nine-month to one-year monastic-type experience in Clayton, Delaware, that was devoted exclusively to prayer and work with only classmates—and in the major seminary was even more focused, as we concentrated primarily on our vocations. In addition to finishing my junior and senior years of college in the first two years of the major seminary (our small class of three students and the class ahead of us took classes at Howard University and The Catholic University, and we received our degrees from Howard), I worked year-round in parishes and in the community (Washington, D.C.), and I went home less often and for much shorter visits. By this time, though, the seminary lifestyle had become ingrained in me, and homesickness rarely entered my mind. Our friendships became stronger, our opinions became more firm, and we even dared to disagree with the system—especially at a time when the country was in turmoil over the Black Power movement and the Vietnam War, and the Catholic Church was losing many of its members.

The social activism of the early 1970s caused me and many of my fellow seminarians to rethink our vocations as some of our views on the social movement in the African American community clashed with those of the Josephite hierarchy. Most decisions to leave (like my own, which I contemplated for an entire year) were self-initiated; but the departures of others who were told to leave by the congregation's higher administration, in large part because of their perceived "radicalism" and unsuitability for the priesthood, precipitated a great deal of the philosophical division that occurred later. Many Black seminarians left the Josephites in the late 1960s and early 1970s, at a time when there was a critical mass of Blacks who were fully convinced that they could still make a contribution to their communities, but without becoming a priest.

Two decades have passed since that time, and it is easy to look back and see that what we predicted did in fact occur—namely, that African American and other Catholics would assume a much greater role in their parishes, and priests would become more subservient to their parish congregations. The latter was a rather bold and controversial prognostication at the time, but most of the signs of the eventual "reformation" (e.g., parish councils, gospel masses, the incorporation of rituals relevant to African Americans, etc.) were already evident. Nevertheless, the seminary experience proved to be a valuable learning opportunity, and many of the men who left have not only been successful in their professional careers but are also active in occupations focused on education and service to the community (e.g., teachers, school and college administrators, professors, social workers, daycare center directors, attorneys, and elected public officials, such as New Orleans's former mayor).

CONCLUSION

It may be coincidental that I find myself today working at Xavier University of Louisiana, the only one of the 104 historically Black colleges that is Catholic, and the only one of 253 Catholic institutions of higher education in the United States that is predominantly Black. But it may also be providential, as I have the opportunity to give something back by working in a Catholic educational environment that has provided so much to the African American community. Catholic schools in the South did more than fill a void: They provided educational opportunities to many African Americans who otherwise would have never had the chance to receive an education. Moreover, the schools operated in spite of tremendous financial obstacles and against public beliefs that Blacks did not need an education. The training and experiences provided to me and many other African Americans in Catholic schools have not only helped to shape us, but they have also provided the foundation for us to be productive in our careers. And while alumni have been successful in every career field across the nation, it has been the commitment to service by most of these alumni that has captured the attention of others who have wondered about the special characteristics of these Catholic schools. As today's educators in public and private schools search for successful practices and interventions, Catholic education models such as the ones described in this chapter deserve to be emulated and studied further.

REFERENCES

Boucree, D. A., & Garibaldi, A. M. (1989). Beating the odds. *Momentum, 20*(1), 303–32.

Brookover, W. (1985). Can we make schools effective for minority students? *Journal of Negro Education, 54*(3), 257–268.

Brookover, W. B., Beady, C., Flood, P., Schweitzer, J., & Wisenbaker, J. (1979). *School social systems and student achievement: Schools can make a difference.* New York: Praeger.

Brookover, W. B., & Lezotte, L. W. (1979). *Changes in school characteristics coincident with changes in student achievement*. East Lansing: Institute for Research on Teaching, Michigan State University.

Detiege, A. M. (1976). *Henriette Delille: Free woman of color.* New Orleans: Sisters of the Holy Family.

CHAPTER 10

I'm Going Home: A Journey to Holy Angels

William Tate

The purpose of this chapter is to provide the reader insight into my experience as a student at Holy Angels. I will say from the outset that the process of writing this chapter was difficult. Elsewhere, I have chronicled important events of my Holy Angels experience (Tate, 1994). Many of my colleagues (both inside and outside the university) have read and responded to the chapter, and their responses have caused me great frustration. Most of them were very gracious with their remarks. "What an interesting story" or "What a different inner-city school" typified their responses to me. Absent from these remarks were the comments and questions that I so desperately sought. No one questioned how this school was able to take African American students from one of the poorest neighborhoods in the United States and educate them. Understand my point here. Many of these same colleagues claim to be "interested" in equity, and some even benefit from research funding awarded to help reform inner-city schools. However, the epistemological boundaries of my colleagues' scholarship—usually derived from psychology—narrow their focus and ultimately their ability to discuss the complexity of the African American school experience (Ladson-Billings & Tate, 1994).

This reality places a heavy burden on African American scholars seeking to improve the school experiences of African American students. We are challenged to expand the boundaries of more traditional educational research to include the voices, experiences, and realities of our lives so that a more comprehensive picture of past educational practice can be provided. Clearly, as a collective, these insights should inform future educational policy and practice. I contend it is very important that our experiences as African American students are not "left at home" when

 ISBN 0-8077-3530-2 (cloth).

we engage in scholarly discussions with colleagues about educational practice.

To help capture my experience, I will draw on methods of the New Race Theory group of legal studies and emerging scholarship in education that incorporates the voices of people of color in order to enact hybridity in academic scholarship (Bell, 1992; Delgado, 1990; Gordon, 1992; Narayan, 1993; Williams, 1991). "Hybridity" is the recognition by scholars of color of the need to depict themselves as minimally bicultural in terms of belonging both to the world of scholars and to a larger society in which race remains a significant factor in how one functions and survives in everyday life (Bell, 1992; Narayan, 1993). Hybridity calls for scholars of color to situate themselves as subjects impacted by everyday experience and professional standards of "scholarship." Scholarship that mixes personal anecdotes, parables, chronicles, stories, poetry, fiction, and revisionist history with rigorous analysis involves enacting hybridity (see e.g., Bell, 1994; Lawrence-Lightfoot, 1994). My intention in this chapter is to provide the reader with such an analysis of my grade school experience.

I begin with a story of a trip back to the community of my youth. My purpose is to provide the reader with important contextual features of the community and Holy Angels. Next, I hypothesize about the undergirding philosophy of Holy Angels school during my tenure. Finally, I provide examples from my experiences that support this hypothesis.

I AM GOING HOME

I exit the Dan Ryan expressway at 35th Street. As I turn east on 35th Street, the new Chicago White Sox park stands in place of the old park of my childhood. For me, the old park represented a warning boundary. West of the park is Bridgeport, the home of Mayor Richard Daley, Sr., during my childhood a haven for lower-middle-class whites who displayed little tolerance for "coloreds." East of the park is the beginning of Chicago's Black Belt.

Proceeding east on 35th Street, I pass by Stateway Gardens, a Chicago Housing Authority project. A recent study reported that Stateway Gardens is the poorest of poor neighborhoods in the United States ("Nation's Poorest Citizens," 1995). Residents at Stateway Gardens had a 1989 per capita income of $1,650, a figure well below the national per capita income poverty level of $3,225.

I wonder what became of my Holy Angels schoolmates who lived in Stateway Gardens. Did they escape these large concrete structures with fenced-in balconies? How little things here have changed—no grass, no playgrounds, and no children. Little adults negotiate this terrain. You see, children can't be children east of White Sox park. To be a child is to die. This reality of my past haunts me as I almost miss the turn onto King Drive.

King Drive, or South Parkway as it was known in 1968, was one of several routes that I traveled to get to Holy Angels. The decision to travel a specific route to and from school was an important one. The local gang activity dictated the path of my journey and that of my schoolmates.

The scenery on this portion of King Drive is dominated by Ida B. Wells, another Chicago Housing Project. After traveling five blocks on King Drive, I turn left onto the former Oakwood Boulevard, which has now been renamed after Father George Clements. In 1969, I was a third grader at Holy Angels when Father Clements assumed responsibility as a priest in our parish. His arrival coincided with the social unrest that marked the end of the 1960s.

The assassination of Dr. Martin Luther King and the riots that followed left the Holy Angels parish and surrounding community to what seemed like a worse economic fate. The loss of Dr. King and the uncertainty of the civil rights movement turned the hopes of many community dwellers to pessimism. However, one source of hope was the leadership of Holy Angels.

THE GUIDING PHILOSOPHY

After completing first grade, I transferred to Holy Angels in 1968 from a nearby public school. A majority of my second-grade classmates were neighborhood children. The composition of the student body when I attended Holy Angels reflects the statistics provided by Shields in Chapter 4. She reports that Holy Angels is not a typical Catholic school or Black Catholic school with respect to enrollment. There are two distinct groups that presently attend the school. The first group is composed of approximately two-thirds of the students, who are from the surrounding community and subsist on fixed incomes. The other group of students are children of Holy Angels graduates. Seventy-five percent of the students accepted to the school are not Catholic.

Many of my classmates would go on to graduate from college. In fact, 80% of Holy Angels graduates become college graduates (Norment, 1986). I hypothesize this success was the result of school leadership built on precepts derived from Black liberation theology.

It is important to note that my hypothesis, like all hypotheses, is an assumption taken to be true for the purpose of argument and investigation. Moreover, it is applied retrospectively from my perspective as a scholar. My intention is to help explain what went on at Holy Angels, rather than suggest that Black liberation theology was the guiding framework of the school leadership. However, I found it very difficult to disentangle my experience at Holy Angels from this philosophy.

Black Liberation Theology Defined

James Cone (1969) described one folkway of American (i.e., United States) society that dated back to the colonial period—racial bonding between the Christian Church and white property owners. His analysis revealed how certain factions within the Christian Church practiced a form of "Christianity" that supported slavery. Cone (1969) stated:

> Slave masters at first forbade the baptism of slaves on the grounds that it was an invasion of their property rights. But the churchmen assured them that there was no relationship between Christianity and freedom in civil matters. (p. 75)

This Eurocentric practice of separating Christian doctrine from freedom in civil matters illustrates how racism was not a series of isolated acts but is endemic in our history, deeply ingrained legally, culturally, and even spiritually (Cone, 1969; Marable, 1983; and Williams, 1991).

Many scholars, educators, and theologians have engaged in critiques of Eurocentric interpretations of Christian doctrine (Cleage, 1972; Frazier, 1974; West, 1982; Woodson, 1933/1990). One response to Eurocentric interpretations of Christian doctrine was the development of a Black liberation theology. Cone (1970) posited:

> In a society where men are oppressed because they are *black*, Christian theology must become *Black Theology*, a theology that is unreservedly identified with the goals of the oppressed community and seeking to interpret the divine character of their struggle for liberation. "Black Theology" is a phrase that is particularly appropriate for contemporary America because of its symbolic power to convey both what whites mean by oppression and what blacks mean by liberation. (pp. 11–12; emphasis in original)

Thus, Black liberation theology is a theology that recognizes the realities of an oppressed community. Moreover, advocates of this theology seek to remedy the oppression.

The Emergence of Black Liberation Theology

Karenga (1993) contended the movement toward a Black liberation theology evolved from several sources. First, it was constructed and implemented in response to the political unrest of the 1960s, with its focus on "Blackness" and social activism. Moreover, this era demanded participation in the Black struggle for liberation and challenged the Church to engage or disband.

Second, Black liberation theology was a response to Martin Luther King, Jr. Karenga (1993) stated:

> King's stress on the social relevance and role of religion and on active engagement in the struggle against social evil were accepted and applied, but his stress on non-violence was challenged or played down, his denunciation of Black power rejected, and his emphasis on redemptive suffering translated as redemption through liberating struggle. (p. 237)

Third, Black liberation theology evolved from an internal push for a more relevant religion in light of the activist tradition of the Black church as well as the social struggle of the era (Cone, 1969, 1970; Karenga, 1993). In part, this process was aided by the political dynamics of the era that forced Black churches to redefine the meaning and role of God in history and the role of God in relation to Black oppression and the fight for liberation.

I will argue for the remainder of this chapter that the Black liberation theology movement had a profound impact on my grade school experience.

THE SCHOOL CONTEXT

Building a Spirit of Determination

Black liberation theology provides a lens to examine how social systems work within the United States. Social conflicts are a function of various factions of society attempting to secure property and property rights over other groups in the allocation of these rewards (e.g., Allen, 1974; Bell, 1992; Marable, 1983). Often hidden or ignored in social conflicts over property and property rights are issues of human rights.

My Holy Angels experience was embedded within the nexus of social conflict. Father George Clements, an activist African American priest, was the pastor of Holy Angels parish. His leadership led to drastic changes in the school structure. For example, he implemented a 12-month school year. Also, he required all parents to participate in a wide variety of community-based events. Yet I contend his most important contribution to my education was the example he set by risking both his career and his life for the struggle to achieve equality for all. (It is not possible in this chapter to discuss the full range of Father Clement's actions. They include, for example, his adoption of children, an act that defied Church law. He also worked to eradicate drugs and gang violence in the community. He continued his efforts despite threats on his life.)

I recall a church service in honor of Dr. Martin Luther King, Jr. A large portrait of the civil rights leader was placed in the church. This portrait replaced one of a canonized saint of the Catholic Church. Sometime later, the school community, including students and parents, were convened for a meeting. Father Clements began the meeting by reading a letter from a higher Church authority. The letter stated that Holy Angels had committed a sacrilegious act by removing the portrait of a saint and replacing it with one of Dr. King. The parish was to remove the portrait of Dr. King from the church and replace it with the portrait of St. James. Failure to switch the portraits would result in Father Clement being suspended from the archdiocese. A major problem with being suspended was that the funding to the school would cease. We were told to think about the letter and that, collectively, a decision would be made by the parishioners.

After the large meeting, my class had a discussion of civil disobedience. We talked about how rights were secured in a democracy. Only through conflict would we have a chance of gaining rights. We used the U.S. struggle for liberation as one frame of reference. Also, the teacher read speeches from Frederick Douglass and other stories of civil rights struggles. The conflict with the archdiocese provided a context in which to discuss a wide variety of other real social issues. Our class session ended with a discussion of the price of acquiring rights. We concluded that gaining and maintaining one's individual rights required a high level of economic independence (i.e., property and property rights).

The school community chose not to follow the archdiocese's request. Subsequently, archdiocese funding was canceled and fundraisers were planned and implemented to support the school. Every student had to support this process by donating time to one or more fundraising events. I learned that there was a price to pay for my rights. However, the price was small in comparison to the denial of basic freedoms. Steele (1992) argues that for too many Black students, "school is simply the place where, more concertedly, persistently, and authoritatively than anywhere else in society, they learn how little valued they are" (p. 78). With this in mind, Holy Angels provides an example of how to empower children with a knowledge of self and a combative spirit of social reform. The result is a student who understands his or her importance to society. It should not be surprising that the church theme of this period was "We got it together by ourselves."

Dealing with Duality

I contend the Holy Angels doctrine of school practice was to prepare students to view the world from the perspective of an African person connected to African people all over the world. This philosophy of education involved locating students within the context of their own cultural references so that they could connect socially and psychologically to other cultures. In education, this means that school administrators and teachers provide students the opportunity to study the world from an African world view. One example from my experience as a Holy Angels student illustrates the school administration's commitment to this approach to education.

It was a typical Thursday afternoon in my fifth-grade class. We would spend this time reviewing for Friday's spelling and vocabulary test. One word on the upcoming spelling test was "raccoon." My teacher, a white male, informed the class that as a child his father referred to raccoons as "coons." By coincidence, my own father, a college student at the time, had recently shared with me Bogle's (1973/1989) analysis of the portrayal of African Americans in films. In his analysis, Bogle describes the "coon" as a group of three variant stereotypes, all designed to portray the African American as an object of amusement—a Black buffoon. At the time of my teacher's remarks, I could only think of the following statement by Bogle (1973/1989):

> The pickaninny was the first of the coon types to make its screen debut. It gave the Negro child actor his place in the black pantheon. Generally, he was a harmless, little screwball creation whose eyes popped, whose hair stood on end with the least little excitement, and whose antics were pleasant and diverting. (p. 7)

I wondered whether my teacher understood the dual meaning of the word "coon." Throughout the school year he had emphasized that some words had several meanings. So I raised my hand and waited. It seemed as if hours passed before he called on me. I informed him and the class that "coon" had another meaning. I went on to describe Bogle's book and the other definition of "coon." It did not take more than a few seconds to recognize that my teacher was quite upset. He asked me to step outside the classroom. Once outside the room, he suggested that I apologize to the class for my remarks. I told him no, that my statement was based on a college book. In my eyes, the college book was more important than our class speller or his father's definition of "coon." I resented the promotion of his father's knowledge over my father's experiences. He sent me to the office. A journey to the office at Holy Angels usually meant some unpleasant form of punishment. I sat in the office next to the school secretary for several minutes. Finally, Father Smith, the school principal, returned to the office. He asked me what I had done to be sent to the office. I explained to him the events that led to my removal from class. He smiled and told me that it was appropriate to point out the dual meaning of the word. In fact, he asked me to retell the story to the school's assistant principal. The assistant principal shook her head in amazement. She suggested that I write a book report on the topic and present it to my class.

Two important events occurred after my discussion with the school's administrators. First, the teacher asked me to prepare and present a report on Bogle's book. Second, the teacher did not return to the faculty the following year. Many years after that incident I talked with Father Smith about several of my former teachers—including my fifth-grade teacher. I inquired why he had left the faculty. Father Smith smiled and said "philosophical differences." I will speculate on the nature of these philosophical differences. I contend that the inability of my teacher to either recognize or discuss the interrelationship between "his" school knowledge, my home experiences, and my experiences in the community as an African American resulted in a tension between the school's philosophy and his "color-blind" approach to education.

My teacher failed to understand an important reality involving the education of African American students. Most of the class understood that as African Americans our lives were valued differently than those of white people. Many of us had been chased out of the bordering neighborhood of Bridgeport after attending White Sox baseball games. We were called a wide assortment of names—including coons. Personally, my mother and I had been denied entry to the Boys Club of Bridgeport, a facility located no more than a mile and a half from my home. How could he stand in front of the class and pretend not to understand that this was a part of our reality? In my eyes, his attempt to provide my class with a "neutral" and color-blind version of the world "delegitimized" his pedagogy. Fortunately, the school's leadership understood the need to staff the school with teachers willing to discuss the interrelationship between school knowledge and our experiences and lived realities as African Americans.

The Curriculum: From Curiosity to Career

Some cognitive theorists suggest that knowledge is constructed through the interaction of the mind and authentic activities (e.g., Brown, Collins, & Duguid, 1989; Resnick, 1987; Walkerdine, 1988). These scholars argue that in-school knowledge is acquired by working alone to memorize rules and solving well-defined problem types. Often, in-school knowledge is narrow and difficult to transfer. In contrast, out-of-school knowledge is acquired by working in an environment to decide the causes of a situation, to solve ill-defined problems, and to construct personal understanding.

Holy Angels attempted to prepare students for both types of knowledge. In-school knowledge is represented by those topics typically found on standard measures of achievement (e.g., the Iowa Test of Basic Skills). We drilled and prepared for standardized testing. Yet this preparation did not include taking practice standardized tests. Instead, the school followed the advice of Carter G. Woodson (1933/1990), whose philosophy continues to provide the structure for the development of multicultural and Africentric curricula in urban schools. We took more mathematics than white students. For example, in sixth grade I was enrolled in three mathematics classes. One class used a traditional textbook series. It was organized and run like most mathematics classrooms—lecture, guided practice, and homework. The second class was designed around a theme of "higher-level thinking skills." This second class consisted of a combination of geometric and algebraic concepts embedded in a wide variety of problem settings. Unlike my more traditional class, this one had no tests, quizzes, or homework. We simply talked about mathematical ideas and concepts. For me, mathematics became a form of verbal communication. This mathematics communication background and preparation has proven to be most useful in my teaching of mathematics and the knowledge conflicts of the academy (e.g., my oral defense in mathematics and mathematics education, professional mathematics presentations, etc.). It was also consistent with recent calls to incorporate mathematics communication into school mathematics (National Council of Teachers of Mathematics, 1989, 1991).

My additional mathematical opportunities extended beyond formal class sessions. I consider these informal opportunities my third mathematics class. These opportunities were critical to the development of my out-of-school mathematical knowledge. For example, my sixth-grade teacher provided the class with a variety of electronic design kits. Instead of going to recess, many students, myself included, opted to work on various electronics projects. In fact, we built a telephone system for the class. The discourse required to complete this project catalyzed our interest in mathematics. How much wire will be needed, given the configuration of the room? How much should we charge for using the phone? The dialogue ranged from economic issues to technical design. Mathematics became real for the class. We were centered in the knowledge-acquisition process and, as a result, we saw ourselves as scientists.

This realistic mathematics experience transferred to my out-of-school life. I was excited about science and mathematics. I made weekly trips to the Museum of Science and Industry. I read scientific journals. I shared my experiences and readings with my classmates, younger brother, and cousin. Today, both my brother and cousin credit my zeal for mathematics for their interest in computers. These childhood interests have moved from intellectual curiosity to their careers in technology-based fields. I say this not to credit myself. Instead, I want to illustrate how good teaching for one student can impact an entire family. My family and friends noticed my interest and that of my brother and cousin. They fed our hunger for science and mathematics with birthday gifts of chemistry sets, microscopes, telescopes, and more books. My school experience helped to catalyze a community of scientific supporters around me. I contend this support would have been different if my school experience consisted mainly of preparing for standardized mathematics tests. Further, my interest in mathematics would have been quite different. How many students talk with their family and friends about the "exciting" class of mathematics test preparation?

FINALLY HOME

I park my car in front of Holy Angels school. The building always seems smaller than I remember. I can't help but stare at the building. I recall very little about the physical design of this building. My memories are of people and events that influenced my life. I will never forget the lectures about leadership from Father Clements. My talks with Father Smith concerning the responsibilities of manhood have been passed on to every young man who will listen to me. I remember the African American leaders who visited our school—Gwendolyn Brooks, Jessie Jackson, and many others—to provide support and counsel.

Unlike my memory of the school building, these events and lessons seem so large in my mind. They have never left me. Perhaps Holy Angels will always be a part of me. That thought feels good. I've never really left home.

REFERENCES

Allen, R. (1974). *Reluctant reformers: The impact of racism on American social reform movements.* Washington, DC: Howard University Press.

Bell, D. (1992). *Faces at the bottom of the well: The permanence of racism.* New York: Basic Books.

Bell, D. (1994). *Confronting authority: Reflections of an ardent protester.* Boston: Beacon.

Bogle, D. (1989). *Toms, coons, mulattoes, mammies, and bucks: An interpretive history of Blacks in American films.* New York: Continuum. (Originally published 1973)

Brown, J. S., Collins, A., & Duguid, P. (1989). Situated cognition and the culture of learning. *Educational Researcher, 18,* 32–42.

Cleage, A. (1972). *Black Christian nationalism.* New York: Morrow.

Cone, J. H. (1969). *Black theology and Black power.* New York: Seabury.

Cone, J. H. (1970). *A Black theology of liberation.* Philadelphia and New York: Lippincott.

Delgado, R. (1990). When a story is just a story: Does voice really matter? *Virginia Law Review, 76,* 95–111.

Frazier, E. F. (1974). *The Negro church in America.* New York: Schocken.

Gordon, B. M. (1992). The marginalized discourse of minority intellectual thought. In C. A. Grant (Ed.), *Research and multicultural education: From the margins to the mainstreams* (pp. 19–31). Washington, DC: Falmer.

Karenga, M. (1993). *Introduction to Black studies.* Los Angeles: University of Sankore Press.

Ladson-Billings, G., & Tate, W. F. (1994, April). *Toward a critical race theory of education.* Paper presented at the American Educational Research Association Annual Meeting, New Orleans.

Lawrence-Lightfoot, S. (1994). *I've known rivers: Lives of loss and liberation.* Menlo Park, CA: Addison-Wesley.

Marable, M. (1983). *How capitalism underdeveloped Black America.* Boston: South End.

Narayan, K. (1993). How native is a "native" anthropologist? *American Anthropologist, 95,* 30–45.

National Council of Teachers of Mathematics. (1989). *Curriculum and evaluation standards for school mathematics.* Reston, VA: Author.

National Council of Teachers of Mathematics. (1991). *Professional Standards for Teaching Mathematics.* Reston, VA: Author.

Nation's poorest citizens living in Chicago housing developments: Study. (1995, February 13). *Jet,* p. 19.

Norment, L. (1986, March 1). One church/One child. *Ebony,* pp. 68–75.

Resnick, L. B. (1987). Learning in school and out. *Educational Researcher, 4,* 13–20.

Steele, C. (1992, April 1). Race and the schooling of Black Americans. *The Atlantic,* pp. 68–78.

Tate, W. (1994). From inner city to ivory tower: Does my voice matter in the academy? *Urban Education, 29,* 245–269.

Walkerdine, V. (1988). *The mastery of reason.* New York: Routledge.

West, C. (1982). *Prophesy deliverance: An Afro-American revolutionary Christianity.* Philadelphia: Westminster.

Williams, P. J. (1991). *The alchemy of race and rights: Diary of a law professor.* Cambridge, MA: Harvard University Press.

Woodson, C. G. (1990). *The mis-education of the Negro.* Trenton, NJ: Africa World. (Originally published 1933)

CHAPTER 11

Topsy Goes to Catholic School: Lessons in Academic Excellence, Refinement, and Religion

Kimberly C. Ellis

I must admit that writing this chapter has been most difficult for me because my Catholic school experiences were more painful than pleasurable, more confusing than clear. In this chapter, I have tried to include detailed accounts of my experiences in the same manner in which I perceived them as a young girl; in addition, I have provided my commentary and/or analysis as a young woman. As a young girl, I sensed that many things were askew; however, I possessed neither the "proper" means of communication nor the "mature" perspective through which to respond. Many times, I felt like an injured baby who, unable to speak the language effectively, could only react with a wild flailing of the arms, loud shrieking, and crying, to everyone's annoyance or dismay. As a young adult, I now have a better understanding of my experiences within the context of the historical period in which I was raised, the period of development (or destruction) of the educational system in the United States, the economic possibilities for the Black community in the 1980s, and the level of understanding that my family and I had of the system of institutionalized racism/white supremacy. Hence, if anyone is to "blame" for my negative educational experiences, neither Catholicism nor Black or white educators in Pittsburgh nor any one school in particular would be liable. Understanding the historicity of racism, however, does not excuse one's behavior, nor does it explain why individuals who are affiliated with institutions plagued by racism remain apathetic and continue the de-

Growing Up African American in Catholic Schools. Copyright © 1996 by Teachers College, Columbia University. All rights reserved. ISBN 0-8077-3530-2 (cloth). Prior to photocopying items for classroom use, please contact the Copyright Clearance Center, Customer Service, 222 Rosewood Dr., Danvers, MA 01923, USA, tel. (508)750-8400.

structive cycle of providing an education that fosters and/or supports this disease.

HOW EXCELLENT IS THY NAME

I grew up on the Hill, an urban Black neighborhood in Pittsburgh, Pennsylvania, and my mother raised me as a Catholic in Saint Benedict the Moor Church. It is funny but not surprising that I did not fully understand the meaning of the word "Moor" (and all of its connotations) until I got to college. I used to wonder why the name of our church sounded so different from others, such as Holy Rosary or Saint Mary Magdalene or Sacred Heart. Why wasn't it simply "Saint Benedict's"? Growing up, I used to hear the phrase "Saint Benedict the Black," but I never knew the deep significance of the word "Moor." Blackness could have simply been a physical description but the word "Moor" signifies an era, an historical place, a social context, and, above all (for me, anyway), a place of origin other than Europe. And besides, why did Saint Benedict's blackness have to stand out from the attributes of the rest of the saints? Why did I not hear of "Saint Joseph the White"? Further, if the blackness of saints of African descent was to be emphasized, was one to assume that all the other saints were White? Even worse, why did I acquire this knowledge in college and not from the bishop, priests, nuns, and members of Saint Benedict the Black? I wondered about these types of issues as a child (lacking, of course, vital historical information) but never gained a clearer understanding of why I was never provided with logical, concrete answers until adulthood. Saint Benedict the Moor Church was one of two Black Catholic churches in Pittsburgh. The other church, Holy Rosary, was one of the few parishes in the United States that had a Black priest. Of course, there was no other Black priest in Pittsburgh, or surely our church would have had him.

Saint Benedict lucked out with Father Louis Vallone, a dark-skinned white priest whose parents had grown up on the Hill. I am not sure if he ever lived on the Hill himself, but Father Vallone possessed such a gift for storytelling and love for children that the parishioners quickly accepted him into the church, and he made it his home. Father Vallone arrived with a little bit of soul, and he left with a whole lot more. He used to praise the children by first asking us if we were being good (as though any of us would have ever 'fessed up to the contrary), and then letting out a slow, deep "veerry gooood" to show his appreciation for our behavior.

Father Vallone always seemed to be on the same level as the parishioners and did not "put on airs." I recognized this even as a teenager. He never kicked out the homeless people who used to wander in the church and walk right up the center aisle during the middle of the mass; he would greet them and invite them to have a seat. He never hurried back to the rectory after mass either; he would always join the congregation for the donuts and coffee served after every 9:30 A.M. mass. When it was time for the Christian Mothers' barbecue, Father Vallone would proudly announce the event and invite everyone to partake of the goodies, but he would proclaim (from the pulpit) that he would be the first in line to get his chicken, ribs, and potato salad and if you didn't arrive in time to get a plate, you couldn't use the "good 'ol Samaritan" line to make him give up his.

Finally, as though his story-tellin', kid-lovin', chicken-eatin' self were not baaad enough—Father Vallone rode a glistening black motorcycle. You could see him cruising up and down the hills on his motorcycle, and if my friends and I saw him, we would yell out, "Father Vallone, we're being goooodd!" When he whisked past us down the hill, we didn't need bionic ears to determine his response over the loud motor. We used to giggle and think about our pastor as cool rider. What priest do you know whose main vehicle of transportation is a motorcycle? Well, how about a deacon? For as long as I can remember, Deacon Dixon, a Black man, was Father Vallone's assistant. I had a general idea of what a deacon's duties entailed, but it seemed as though Deacon Dixon did so much more than just "assist." He served as a father figure for me, especially because my father had already passed away when I was 9 years old and my mother never remarried. I really liked Father Vallone, and I am sure he knew of the importance of Black role models for Black children, which is why most of the positions of power within the church were held by Black people. Deacon Dixon lived in the rectory, which was right next to Saint Benedict the Moor School, so I saw him just about every day. He always welcomed me and gave me plenty of hugs. And he was another cool rider. Seeing him and Father Vallone get on their motorcycles and ride away was a sight to see. They looked like the Dynamic Duo. Unfortunately, Deacon Dixon (peace be upon him) was killed in a tragic motorcycle accident during my teenage years. A closed casket was necessary for the funeral since the accident left him dismembered and maimed; luckily, my last memories of him entail bear hugs, a rough beard, and big smiles.

I loved the family I had at Saint Benedict's. Although I was not primarily concerned with the specifics of Catholicism during my childhood, the communal spirit that existed within and throughout the church community was like no other I had ever witnessed in any Catholic church. Holding hands while singing the "Our Father" as a congregation, as opposed to simply listening to the choir sing, was a personal favorite of mine. So was prolonging the service with an interlude of "peace time." Hugs were exchanged, as well as brief checkups on family members, and personal conversations with Father Vallone were a common sight and a blessed one. We seemed to have the "best of both worlds," so to speak, since the Catholic church was so highly esteemed and yet known to usually be so boring. But we members of Saint Benedict's not only had our own gospel choir, we had the prestigiousness of a Catholic reputation along with the "down-homeness" of a Baptist congregation. I was shocked to find out that the majority of other Catholic masses lasted only 45 minutes.

I had always felt that Father Vallone could relate to Black people so well because he had grown up poor and had also faced discrimination; in addition to facing classism, perhaps he faced discrimination because he was darker than most whites. You could not have told me that he didn't have any Black people in his family. And yet, when I saw his parents, they were quite white-looking. On a hot summer day, one might have thought Father Vallone was a light-skinned Black man.

Coming out of a movie theater recently with one of my best friends, Lisa Picken, we spotted Father Vallone. I had not seen him in years, not since he was assigned to another church (in a predominantly white community). Besides, I had chosen to move away from Catholicism and experiment with other belief systems since entering college. We were so happy to see him, and we set him up to say, "Very gooood"—and he did. Looking older, but in good condition, Father Vallone reminded me of the fondness I had felt for my church family as a child. Believe it or not, at his age, he was still riding a glistening black motorcycle. Watching him ride off again made me feel more assured that, although I had left the Catholic faith, my church family, including Father Vallone would never depart.

AIN'T MISBEHAVIN'

The comforting feeling I felt at church was not the same feeling I had at school. Having attended public school through the second grade, I was ill-prepared for the emotional rigors of Catholic school. A state of bewilderment, paranoia, and self-doubt riddled my five years at Saint Benedict the Moor grade school, beginning in the third grade. Although I was no angel, I was not a brat, either. Ironically, I might have been considered a role model for other students, but I was characterized as the "smart girl with a bad attitude." Winning awards in spelling bees, receiving countless annual academic awards, and being an all-A student did not counter the fact that I missed getting awards for perfect attendance because of the number of suspensions I accumulated over the years. Being much too young to understand the irony of my situation in grade school, I can now reflect upon the misgivings of my Catholic school experiences and provide better insight than my written record might indicate.

Corporal punishment was still an acceptable means of discipline when I entered the third grade in 1981. It was my understanding that all of the students were allowed to be spanked, but the harsher punishment was to be paddled by Sister Margery, the school principal. She had a long, thick wooden paddle; it scared one simply to see it propped up against the wall behind her desk. On the other hand, there was "Mister Almighty," the yardstick named by Mrs. Viola Burgess, my fourth-grade teacher.

Believe me, I had my fair share of shakings, hand smacks, and spankings, but my mother swore I was an angel throughout the entire year. What or whom was the big difference? The administrator. Mrs. Viola Burgess was a petite, Black woman from Mississippi (and a Baptist, at that). All the students were afraid of her; I suspect some of the other teachers were afraid of her, too. The differences between her and the other teachers were so plentiful that my fearful anxiety quickly dissipated, while comfort, admiration, and inspiration ensued. Well, all right, the fear remained, to some extent, but for different reasons.

Mrs. Burgess treated all her students as though we were her own children. There was a certain caring in her eyes that went beyond that of the other teachers, lay or Catholic. When she corrected me for misbehaving, she was much harsher and stricter than Sister Ernestine (a known tough one), but it was easy to submit to her authority because she allowed me to maintain a sense of dignity and pride. Her respect for me was evident in that she simply reminded me who the adult was and that I had a lot to learn. And she was adamant about her children being in school to learn and not simply to be baby-sat or merely tolerated.

If you were present in Mrs. Burgess's class and did not have your homework the next day, you had earned your automatic spanking. Most of the time, she used her hand or a small ruler and smacked the inside of your palm (thank God for calluses). If you were really misbehaving, she called upon Mister Almighty, or worse yet, she took off her own belt. I hated the way she would grab your skirt and pull it to one side, to make sure there was only one layer of clothing between her strike and your body. For the boys, she would use their belt hoops to stretch the fabric across, leaving no space for any rebellious or sympathetic threads to shelter those puny buttocks. She wanted to make sure you captured the essence of the punishment, and, if you moved, the lick didn't count. Oh, the tyranny that existed in those days!

Most of my troublesome periods came not during class time but during the transition periods in the hallways, during lunchtime, and after school. My mother was thrilled that I continued getting all A's and had only a few mishaps. Woe, if my gluteus maximus could talk! Mrs. Burgess wondered why she always had to chastise me for things that occurred outside the classroom when I rarely "acted up" in her classroom. What neither of them understood was that Mrs. Burgess had already won my undying love, respect, and loyalty and she could do no wrong in my eyes. Her caring was sincere, and her inspiration was relentless. She pushed me further than any other teacher had in the past; her goals for me were so high that I looked forward to every challenge.

The administration of her rules and punishments varied greatly from those of her colleagues. Her classroom had a unique set of rules, which allowed for a degree of freedom and individuality. When I blurted out an answer to a question in class and laughed about the topic at hand with another classmate, she encouraged my participation and either explained my misconceptions or confirmed my correct answers. My other teachers would stop the class and correct me for not using the proper volume and inflection, remind me to raise my hand before speaking, and then call on somebody else since I had broken protocol. Usually, I would then have to wait for the rest of the class to give all the wrong answers until I might be called on again to give the correct one.

Has anyone ever seen a child's spirit sink and finally die? More often than not in school, it is teachers who are doing the killing. Children are supposed to giggle and contemplate and shake their hands ferociously in the air until they are called upon. Most of the nuns (who were all white) seemed to correct me for the sake of maintaining order. It seemed as if the rules were the most important aspect of our education, and not the education itself. Was it a life lesson to make sure that no matter how rigid the rules of the school, one would always follow them—as preparation for maintaining social order through obedience to law? Rules were to be blindly followed, never questioned, and their limitations within the punishment /obedience stage of development were not evident or relevant.

Most of Mrs. Burgess's instruction was interactive, which made our learning more interesting and deterred bad behavior. She never had to beg me to participate in class discussions because I loved learning and loved learning in her class. Instructors tend to appreciate enthusiastic and energized students in the classroom, which is why my participation was most commonly an asset rather than a liability. Fortunately, I was placed in the Scholars' Program, a consortium of schools in which advanced, weekly instruction was given away from one's home school. Here, in a public school, learning was less rigid and more individualized. This program supplemented our education with academic and creative endeavors that Saint Benedict's couldn't afford to provide. However, an integral aspect of my education as a Black child was missing until I reached the fourth grade.

Academically, one of the major differences between Mrs. Burgess's curriculum and that of every other teacher at Saint Benedict's was that she included lessons on African American history. Memorizing "Lift Every Voice and Sing," the Black national anthem written by James Weldon Johnson, was mandatory. We learned this song first, and then we opened up our Black history books. Resembling every other history book, with questions at the end of each chapter, the only difference between our books and those of our peers was that ours were filled with the names and faces of people who looked just like us. Our weekly lessons began in September and carried us through June. Every Thursday—not just in February—we were introduced to a new name, a new face, and another achiever against the odds. We paid tribute to Carter G. Woodson, the original designer of Black History Month, by staging a theatrical production for the rest of the school. We did not simply talk about our history—we had to become our heroes and heroines by assuming their dress, speech, and action, much as one may see white youngsters portraying Abraham Lincoln and George Washington in their own school plays. Parents and community members attended our productions in droves, which made us feel doubly important. Memories of one of my peers playing Jesse Jackson and proclaiming, "It's time for a Black man to live in the White House," and of another, adorned with sequins and flowers, playing Vanessa Williams, newly crowned as Miss America 1983 and waving at the crowds, remain vivid in my mind. The fourth grade was mostly responsible for the Black History Month production, while other grades were responsible for Christmas shows, Spring Flings, and so on. While I loved performing and learning about other Black people, I did not understand the full impact this type of extended curriculum would have on me until my senior year in high school.

Mrs. Burgess was the only teacher, throughout my entire primary education, who attempted to provide a full curriculum for Black history, despite the school's limited resources. She did not simply pay lip service to our competence and importance; she made us look within by holding up a mirror of accomplishment to our faces. Thus knowledge through experience proved better than knowledge as theory. Because she embodied that which she taught—pride, discipline, achievement, integrity—I was able to learn by her example as well as through what was written between the covers of our books. She was a spiritual woman who guided me in directions that my lessons in Catholicism would never take me.

OVER THE FOREST AND THROUGH THE WOODS

In stark contrast to my previous school year, "all hell broke loose" during the fifth grade. My father died a few weeks before my October 17 birthday, my grandmother had been diagnosed with lung cancer, my behavior grew worse, and I was up to my third suspension by the beginning of March, which meant a possible expulsion. I can remember sitting in the conference room waiting to serve yet another detention when Sister Kathy, my fifth-grade teacher, came in and kneeled down beside my chair. She asked me why I kept misbehaving and told me that the principal was getting ready to write my expulsion letter and call my mother that week. She asked me what was going on in my life, and I calmly looked at her and said, "Well, Sister Kathy, my grandmother is dying." She looked taken aback by my response, collected herself, and asked for more details. To be honest, I was using my grandmother's illness as an excuse based on my fear. Getting kicked out of school would have brought the wrath of my mother upon me, and I already felt sorry for her because she had lost her husband and now she was watching her mother die six months later. Children's grandparents die all the time, and I had not considered elderly people's deaths to be "a big deal" because everyone knew they had to go sometime, but, as I related the details of my year to Sister Kathy, I began to realize, Hey, maybe this *is* why I've been acting up in class! My grandmother lived two houses up from us on Bedford Avenue. I never considered the possibility that I was also experiencing stress because I depended upon my grandmother every day after school. My mother always had two or three jobs, and now that my grandmother was sick, I was becoming more and more of a latchkey kid. Talking to Sister Kathy was cathartic.

Her reaction was so profound, I started to feel as if I had just told another lie to get out of a sticky situation. See, it was neither my father's nor my grandmother's death that was so frightening. It was how their deaths were a major impact upon my mother. She and I were so close before the tragic reality of their deaths; I told my mother everything that happened in school, showed her all my papers, and boasted about my grades. She brought me treats home from work and I always got a new Encyclopedia Brown book every two weeks. I was losing my mother to the face of death. I needed some serious attention and knew just how to get it. I knew Sister Kathy did not understand my pain, but her empathy touched my soul.

Still kneeling in that conference room when I ended my story, Sister Kathy asked me if I would mind if she came to my grandmother's house and said a prayer for her. At first I thought this was a test. I figured that she was feigning concern, as mean as I perceived Sister Kathy to be. I had witnessed her harshness and cruelty before, for example, the day David Dunn decided to get creative while looking for his pen on the floor. He had been crawling around on his knees searching for his pen under a few desks, but when he found it, he continued to crawl around, steadily poking calves and sneaking peeks under the girls' uniform skirts. Sister Kathy walked back into the room and saw him, so he jumped up and started for his desk. She beckoned him toward her and instructed him to get back down on his hands and knees. All of the students were chuckling because we thought David would have to maintain that position for a while. But when David assumed the position, Sister Kathy drew back her foot and then kicked him, fiercely, on his buttocks. David's body flew forward, and he landed on his face. Having witnessed this vile behavior as well as many similar instances, it was hard for me to imagine that Sister Kathy could have my best interests at heart. But not only did she come home with me, she walked with me during my entire route home. I was so impressed. I had never seen any of the nuns walking through my neighborhood, and I even had to pass four or five blocks of projects to get to my house. And this white woman was willing to literally walk in my footsteps.

By the time we got to my grandmother's house, Sister Kathy became the little present that I was giving to my grandmother. She stood in the living room over my grandmother's deathbed (by this time, Mommy had rented one of those hospital beds that one gets when the end is fast approaching and one wants to die at home) and talked with her. After their conversation, Sister Kathy held her hand and said a prayer. Before Sister Kathy left, I took a peek at my grandmother's face. She looked so grateful and peaceful, I thanked God that I had been so close to expulsion. I walked Sister Kathy to the door and asked her if she wanted me to walk back up the hill with her. She said, "No, I'll be fine, and I'll see you in school tomorrow." She seemed like such a different person walking up that hill by herself. I never knew how it was that I was not expelled from school, but I can only imagine that she had something to do with it. I was to learn later, from a former teacher, that part of the reason why both my brother and I were not expelled from Saint Benedict was because we were Catholic. After that year, Sister Kathy was transferred, and I have not seen her since, but I always wanted to thank her for that single act of kindness.

The sixth through the eighth grades were not as dramatic, although I definitely had memorable experiences. Fortunately and unfortunately, Mrs. Burgess did not allow me to say good-bye completely to the fourth grade. I had become a favorite of hers, probably because I was one of her biggest challenges, and she continued to "guide me" all the way up through eighth-grade graduation. In fact, many teachers would simply report my behavior to her, and they would purposefully give me detention on Mrs. Burgess's rotation days for monitoring detention hour. After a few more spankings, her nurturing lectures about my potential finally began to sink in. I ended up graduating from Saint Benedict the Moor and moved on to Saint Paul's Cathedral High School.

ONE WOMAN'S HEAVEN IS ANOTHER ONE'S HELL

The irony of my experiences at Saint Paul's Cathedral High School is that I am the one who chose to enter that institution. My mother had given me a choice of which high school I could attend. I was so sick of nuns by the time I got out of Saint Benedict's, I just knew I would choose Schenley High School, a public school whose advanced students were known for their academic achievement. But when I visited Schenley, the chaos of the public school system scared me, and smelling marijuana smoke in the locker room sealed my fate for Saint Paul's Cathedral.

One series of experiences that I would be remiss to leave out of these reflections are my trials and tribulations with the Spanish teacher I shall call Senora. During the first few days of freshman frenzy, I used to catch her watching me walk down the halls and heard later, from another student, that she had asked, "Who's that tall, pretty Black girl?" Standing a full 5 feet and 9 inches in ninth grade, it wasn't hard for me to stand out, but her compliments about my height and beauty made me feel a bit uneasy, especially because I ended up in her class.

Senora seemed to wait until I turned to another student to tell me to be quiet, even while other students were talking. She would purposefully not call on me in class even when she knew I had the correct answers. If I complained about something in the texts, she responded harshly or with ambivalence. When I got my tests back, she took points off for minor things that she rarely paid attention to in class, such as accent marks and word choice. When I expressed my disappointment with my grade, her response was disrespectful. The look in her eyes suggested that she was pleased to give me less than the A that I expected. Somehow my grade dropped to a D in her class within one month. After bouts of balling up her detention slips, countless verbal battles, and having Senora exclaim,

"Stop staring at me like that—go to the office," the semester ended with a major conference between the principal, the dean of discipline, my mother, and myself, along with thirteen other classmates, all present to attest to Senora's psychotic behavior toward me in the classroom. She ended up leaving the school because we merged with Sacred Heart to become Oakland Catholic High School and Senora was not invited back to teach. I was told to seek counseling and that the D was still on my report card.

Although one did not have to do much to get in trouble in a Catholic school, I never seemed to break any of the major rules. It was all the little ones that got me. I hated the fact that our socks had to be off-white when off-white socks were so hard to find in stores. When I complained about this, we were told by Mrs. Hammill, our principal, to dip our white socks into tea in order to dye them. In addition, we were chastised for wearing white thermal underwear to protect our naked legs. Above all, I hated being and feeling "watched," as though someone were just waiting for me to step out of line. On the other hand, I am not trying to portray myself as a student who never did anything wrong and remained trapped by "the system." What I am suggesting is that I did not do anything remotely different from what any of the other students at Saint Paul's did (I passed notes, gossiped, and played practical jokes), and yet I seemed to suffer the severest punishments, in order to set an example for other students. Make no mistake about it, I was a leader, but one too immature to take on such a heavy burden as being solely responsible for the behavior of the students in the junior class. Whereas the white students were warned about their behavior before being punished, I would receive an instant detention. There was a deep level of hypocrisy and racism at Saint Paul's, and I witnessed it firsthand. I began to feel as though I were suffocating and I could not wait to be able to breathe fresh air again.

Wise children do not get dumber with age and Black children can sense when they are not wanted. This is not simply a "Black thing," however, because there were other Black students in my class who followed all the rules, were content, and never had any major problems at Saint Paul's. There was just something about my spirit that was unsettling for some people. Perhaps I possessed the spirit of the revolting slave who would do anything to free herself from oppression and refused to play "the monkey for the honky," as my friend Terra used to say. I could not help the fact that I was almost 6 feet tall, that I did not shuffle my feet when I walked, that I didn't mumble or show slight, nervous smiles as I passed by authority figures. Highly active, I had the type of energy that should not be stifled. This does not mean I did not know how to obey rules or listen to authority. After all, I respected those who respected me—even in the fourth grade, despite all the authority Mrs. Burgess represented, she was never disrespectful to us. Moreover, my mother had instilled a sense of pride in me—I would not allow myself to go to school looking unkempt or unruly. I felt as though I were being treated as a slave (as much as I knew about slavery at the time) who needed to be seasoned to humbly submit to a system of mindless laws and practices. Each unjust detention felt like a whip across my back, while I curled my body in the fetal position to protect my soul. I could not fully comprehend nor realize my potential at Saint Paul's because of this environment. I imagine that it was only my friends, family, and church community that allowed me to survive during this period. I had tossed ideas of suicide around in my head when situations reached their lowest point and my mother did not believe my accusations—they seemed so absurd.

Sister Jeanne, the guidance counselor, was the only adult at Saint Paul's whom I felt I could trust to any considerable degree. If you saw Sister Jeanne walking down the street, you would never guess that she was a nun. Her nails were always done in a sharp style and they always stayed polished, her clothes were respectable but stylish, she wore sassy high-heeled shoes, and she had the loudest, most obnoxious laugh I had ever heard. And all of the students loved her. Sister Jeanne was a rebel in her own right. She was the most individual nun I had ever met, and yet she did not seem any less connected with God than any of the other nuns. Her office had a sofa, a rug, and two coffee tables with a variety of magazines on both tables. Any student could go and hang out with Sister Jeanne.

Clarifying why Senora has such a major problem with me, it was Sister Jeanne who told me that I had an aura about me that was so different from that of many other students. She explained that my high-spiritedness instantly attracted people who wanted to follow me. She told me that I had a reigning confidence and that my laughter would carry me throughout life. She indicated that the power struggle was based on envy and realized that Senora did not know how to deal with someone like myself because I represented something she had always wanted to be but wasn't. So that's where all the "tall and pretty" compliments came from; no wonder I felt so uneasy.

Sister Jeanne did not succumb to or accept other teachers' perceptions of me, perhaps because she heard many different stories from a variety of people and somewhere inside the collage was the truth. But why didn't she speak to me? Why didn't she tell me? I would have felt so much better knowing that she was "on my side" despite anyone else. Perhaps she felt the pressures of the institution and did not want to risk her status for me. An unjust system (particularly institutionalized racism/white supremacy) forces individuals within the system to willfully or unwillfully play a role in suppressing the spirit of the Black child. Nevertheless, it was Sister Jeanne who told me that I had truly grown to be a woman and that I had "flowered into my own" during my senior year. And it was true. Developing Black Awareness Week during my senior year served as the beginning stages of my rite of passage into Black womanhood. To this day, I remain amazed and grateful to the Creator for guiding me in the right direction. My fourth-grade lessons in Black history provided positive self-images and the knowledge that someone who looks just like me can achieve. These lessons gave me strength during periods of confusion. I learned, years later, that Mrs. Burgess had taken it upon herself to teach us Black history and had the books ordered. That part of the curriculum had not been institutionalized, and we did not receive a grade in Black history. A crucial part of my development had been stunted since no other academic arena offered the history of my people for the next 10 years. A seed had been planted in the fourth grade; all I needed was a little more water.

LIGHT AND HONOR HAVE ARRIVED

During my senior year at Oakland Catholic (we had merged by now), I was in seventh heaven. Senora was gone, Mrs. Hammill was gone, new teachers were hustled in, and Sacred Heart students seemed ambivalent and still angry that their school had not been chosen as the base for the merger. There was so much confusion surrounding this new school. I was lost in the shuffle. I felt like a regular student until Black Awareness Week. Of course, one may ask why I was not nourished by role models, such as Charles Lwanga, a patron saint whose statue stood tall inside the chapel in my grade school, and Saint Benedict the Moor, for whom the church and school were named. Considering the power of images, however, it should be understood that any Black child who is bombarded with pictures of a white Jesus, a white Mary, an abundance of white saints, and, in fact, a white God will not be able mentally to place two Black saints in any order of importance. To this day, above the altar in Saint Benedict the Moor Church (which stands on Freedom Corner in Pittsburgh), there remains a huge, three-dimensional structure of a white, Santa Claus-lookin', blue-eyed, pale-skinned, blond-haired God holding up His white Son, Jesus, on a crucifix with little, white angels flying about Him while playing the harp. My mother taught me that I was a child of God and made in His image. How was I supposed to accept these images in my church every Sunday as a Black child and grow up mentally balanced?

By being told that Jesus' color doesn't really matter? If it doesn't really matter, then why can't He be Black? Further, on the basis of historical evidence, the one color that Jesus could *not* have been is the one color he is most often portrayed to be. A mental revolution was bound to take place, and this revolution occurred during the organization of Black Awareness Week at Oakland Catholic High School.

One of my friends, Sherri, and I were at lunch discussing our disgust at the fact that February was only a few days away and we saw nothing being prepared to celebrate Black History Month. Hence, we grappled with plans to celebrate all 28 days and ran to discuss our plans with a few teachers. We were directed to Ms. Celene Scamen, the vice principal, who appeared shocked to see me in her office without a detention slip. Excitedly and often interrupting each other, Sherri and I described our plans, sure that permission would be granted to execute them. Ms. Scamen told us that she would have to discuss our plans with the principal, Sister Claudia Klyn, and that they would meet with us again. I figured that she had to go to the higher authority only because we were asking for a few all-school assemblies, which required more than a mere nod of the head. When we were called back into the office, however, I began to realize exactly what I would be up against. The first excuse for not having anything at all was because we should have come earlier; then came the excuse that Black history did not have to be celebrated in February and that March would be just as good a month as any. Next, we were told that there were too many scheduled masses and other assemblies to conduct, which would make it impossible to hold any more. On the other hand, we were free to decorate the halls. I began to feel slighted, taken advantage of, and I felt ashamed of both Ms. Scamen and Sister Claudia. I think I was ashamed of them because I had finally begun to understand what institutionalized racism was all about.

I became indignant and adamant about having an all-school assembly, because we assembled other times for what I deemed "stupid" reasons. Preparation for California Achievement Tests, corny contests, and talent shows could not measure up to the recognition of an entire people. I knew if I let them explain away my history so easily, I would leave that office feeling diminished and worthless. The more adamant I became, the closer I got to the real truth as to why we could not have any all-school assemblies honoring Black History Month. Finally, and I could not believe it, Sister Claudia Klyn, the principal of my entire high school, let the words fall out of her mouth: "I don't think the girls are ready for this." I wanted to scream. What the hell did she think I had been ready for all these years? And I knew that "the girls" meant "the white girls." Plainly, the white girls were not ready for all of this Black stuff. Sister Jeanne privately encouraged me to continue pressing the administration to accept Black Awareness Week, and after I threatened to use the media to taint Oakland Catholic's reputation, Sister Claudia and I reached a compromise—time would be allotted for two all-school assemblies, along with a designated time period (albeit a shorter one) to teach Black history outside of the assemblies. Hence, we had what I called Black Awareness Week.

Black Awareness Week was a huge success. So many teachers humbly admitted just how little they had known about Black history. They were also surprised at how well the program was presented and expressed their admiration of the organization of the all-school assemblies. Little did they know that we received very little help from the administration and that Sherri had left my side after the major controversy began. I encouraged the younger Black students to do their research at home and in the library, from which they had to produce two or three Black achievers from different fields. In addition to such people as George Washington Carver and Harriet Tubman, we did presentations on Toni Morrison, Edmonia Lewis, and Paul Robeson. The success of Black Awareness Week, however, didn't consist of teachers' comments alone. My fatigue from weeks of gathering information, making decorations, and rehearsing was transformed into a deep sense of pride upon seeing so many students, Black and white, work together to develop an outstanding production. The example of Black Awareness Week was the most truthful and realistic sign of cultural pride, respect, and interracial unity that I had ever seen during my four years in high school.

AND STILL I RISE

Many times it seems as though my Catholic school experiences consisted of a series of failures due to the way I was treated. In all fairness, I must acknowledge that I have Sister Ernestine to thank for the spelling bee rehearsals, Sister Kathy for visiting my grandmother, Sister Christy for teaching me the basics of English, Sister Jeanne for having faith in me when very few teachers did. These are people who, considering their limitations, overextended themselves to help me in some way or another. One of my heroines was and still is Mrs. Viola Burgess, whom I must thank for her love, guidance, positive image, and persistence.

On graduation day, in May 1990, my tears watered my bouquet of roses as I walked up the church aisle of Saint Paul's Cathedral to take my seat. The release of anxiety, the accomplishment, and the relief that I felt knowing that I would never have to step foot through these doors again, unless I wanted to, were overwhelming. Many onlookers smiled as they concluded that I was sad about leaving my friends and beloved teachers. But I knew otherwise.

The mental and emotional trauma that I had to deal with throughout my primary education attests not only to the travesty of a Eurocentric school system for a Black child, the hypocrisy of some of our Catholic institutions, and the stifling effects of ignorant and unsympathetic teachers but also to the failure of the American educational system as a whole. Now that public schools have failed Black children so miserably, Catholic schools seem more appealing than ever with their notions of "academic excellence." But while I did receive a quality education (for the most part), it was no different from and in many ways inferior to that of students in the public school systems who participated in the honors program.

I would not suggest that Catholic schools are the answer for today's Black American child. Catholic schools remain a part of a system that does not have the best interests of the Black child in mind. No child, Black or white, should be relegated to the likes of my experience, but the pattern becomes cyclical when individuals do not choose to take a stand.

There are positive lessons that I learned from my experiences, as there is the possibility of hope in every negative situation. I have learned how my faith in the Creator should be steadfast and strong for making all things possible and for showing me my job on this earth. I have learned that African people can adapt to any environment, whether uplifting or oppressive, and can still grow and achieve. And not only do we achieve but we surpass mainstream standards.

I feel a sense of failure about many of my experiences in Catholic schools because I cannot help but imagine how my potential would have been realized if I had been nurtured in a spiritually encouraging, mentally uplifting, and caring institutional environment. I had always felt like an outcast in school, but of a different sort than those who may be social outcasts if they choose to pierce their navels or dye their hair purple. I was an institutional outcast, rejected by the foundation upon which the institution was built. I can only imagine where I might be today if I had more Black teachers as role models, a Black Jesus, and an encouraging and more challenging curriculum that encompassed my wholeness as a person. I celebrate who I am today because my mother has always told me, "Honey, they can take everything away from you, but your education is something that no one can take away once you obtain it." The depth of my mother's desire for me to get a good education was enough for me to survive, but I do not want Black children, or any children for that matter, to simply survive. I want them to thrive, succeed, and maintain excellence.

I graduated from Emory University in 1994 and will receive my master's degree from the University of Connecticut in 1996. After obtaining my doctorate, I hope to start an independent school for Black students. I pray that God will give me the wisdom, guidance, and knowledge to provide for these children above and beyond that which I wished for myself. The struggle continues, and still we shall rise.

NOTE

The name Topsy in the title of this chapter refers to a character in Harriet Beecher Stowe's novel, *Uncle Tom's Cabin.* She was characterized as a wild, implike child with a strange sense of humor and deemed uneducable; when asked why she could not behave, she proclaimed, "I guess it's 'cause I'se so wicked!" She was the one slave none of the whites could control, no matter how many times she was whipped or beaten. Topsy was someone for whom society did not find a place until she was taught how to read the Bible, which she took with her when she became a missionary in Africa, where she could at last live freely.

CHAPTER 12

Lessons Learned: Implications for the Education of African Americans in Public Schools

Jacqueline Jordan Irvine

The failure of African American students to achieve in America's public schools is well documented. On every indicator of academic achievement, such as the SAT, the National Assessment of Educational Progress, and college attendance, African American students' performance lags behind that of their white and Asian peers (Irvine, 1990; Jaynes & Williams, 1989; Quality Education for Minorities Project, 1990).

There have been many strategies and interventions aimed at reversing this cycle of school failure, including but not limited to desegregation, compensatory programs such as Head Start, magnet schools, higher standards with more stringent accountability systems, longer school days and longer school years, charter schools, Levin's accelerated schools, Comer schools, and an Afrocentric curriculum. Although these reforms have produced some increased performance on standardized test scores, the score gains and other measures of school achievement have been relatively small and inconsistent over time.

Inspired by the works of Jones (1981), Sowell (1976), and Siddle Walker (1993), the perspectives offered in this volume contextualize the school achievement of African Americans by examining schools (in this case, Catholic schools) that have a demonstrated record of educating African American students from a variety of social classes and from big cities and small towns across this country. The volume has critically reviewed the education of African Americans in Catholic schools through a variety

 ISBN 0-8077-3530-2 (cloth). Prior to photocopying items for classroom use, please contact the Copyright Clearance Center, Customer Service, 222 Rosewood Dr., Danvers, MA 01923, USA, tel. (508)750-8400.

of methods to provide contemporary insights on critical elements that are necessary for the school achievement of African American students.

Intended not merely as a cursory and/or laudatory treatment of academic excellence in Catholic schools, the historical pieces, the case study, and personal memoirs reveal examples of cultural incongruity, denial of cultural heritage, silenced voices, marginalization of racial identity, strict and often unreasonable discipline, and religious proselytization. The chapters are also persuasive stories of achievement, race consciousness, resistance, biculturalism, malleability, empowerment, and adaptation.

The subtle and recurring messages that inform the current education of African Americans in public schools are perhaps the most significant contribution of the book. These messages are organized under three themes: (1) curriculum and instruction, (2) common values and shared visions, and (3) race and racial identity.

CURRICULUM AND INSTRUCTION

Franklin reminds us in his chapter that when African Americans joined the Catholic faith they did so because of the reputation of its schools, which charged low tuition and produced high-quality graduates. Polite, Garibaldi, Tate, Foster, and York tell us that the nature of the curriculum in Catholic schools was structured, college preparatory, traditional, and demanding. While attending Holy Angels in the early 1970s, Tate had three math classes in the sixth grade and exposure to science and technology that inspired his current professional career and interests. As early as the late 1950s, Foster and I were introduced to languages such as French, Latin, and Greek as well as art, music, and the theater. Ellis, a 1990 Catholic school graduate, suggests that this high-status curriculum may not currently be sustained. She laments that her curriculum was not rigorous and thought that her peers in honors courses in public schools had a more challenging curriculum.

Before the civil rights movement, the curriculum was academic, highly structured, and overwhelmingly Eurocentric. York's chapter reveals that during the late nineteenth century, Catholic parish schools for immigrants reflected the cultural as well as religious influences of the parishioners. Yet Delpit says that her introduction to Africa in her Catholic school was the collection of money "to send to poor pagan children of Africa." Franklin found that African American Catholic schools were designed to "expose their pupils to the prevailing white American Catholic culture and tradition." Tate's description of Holy Angels and Polite's description of the present St. Frances Academy suggest that Catholic schools are currently attempting to infuse aspects of African American literature, history, and culture into the curriculum. However, Ellis describes the "travesty of a Eurocentric curriculum" and emphasizes that her most pleasant experience in Catholic schools occurred in the classroom of an African American lay teacher who insisted her students learn and exposed them to and helped them to appreciate their history.

As for the pedagogy in Catholic schools, there is overwhelming evidence that it was traditional and "unremarkable." Shields's case study described Holy Angels teachers as "having no special pedagogy." Delpit calls the teaching style "didactic," and Foster describes it as "unenlightened." It appears that the Catholic school teachers were either unaware of or unimpressed with the educational research on how children learn and how they should be taught. As confirmed in the studies of Bryk, Lee, and Holland (1993), Catholic teachers are "ordinary," yet the degree of engagement by their students was and continues to be very high. There is an interesting parallel between the teaching styles of African American teachers in segregated schools pre-*Brown* and Catholic school teachers. In an ethnographic work about a segregated school in North Carolina, Siddle Walker (1993) documented that African American teachers' success was related to their interpersonal caring rather than to a particular method or teaching style. She states that "the method appeared to be insignificant." The works of Sowell (1976), Jones (1981), and Baker (1982) support Siddle Walker's observations.

COMMON VALUES AND SHARED VISIONS

The naive interpretation of this publication is that it is an attestation to differences. On the contrary, there is overwhelming evidence that there existed a strong set of clearly articulated, accepted values embraced by the Catholic school educators, their students, and their mostly working-class or poor non-Catholic parents. Delpit calls this phenomenon "the seamlessness between home and school." Some of these values included discipline and order, a sense of mission and purpose that is morally based, high expectations, and an understanding of the centrality of parents and family in the education of their children.

Both the personal memoirs and the case studies of Holy Angels and St. Frances Academy emphasize the values of order and discipline. In comparison to public schools, there was no tolerance for major or minor misbehaviors such as talking back, questioning authority, missed homework, or aggression. The teachers, both lay and religious, were committed not only to their students' academic development but also to their character and spiritual development. Teachers were mission-oriented and believed that academic achievement and deference and obedience to secular and sacred law were indistinguishable and equally important goals.

From the perspective of the African American students who attended Catholic schools, the mission of character development was most likely remembered by them because they were subjected to frequent and unrelenting use of corporal punishment that was administered to enforce and sustain the values of discipline and order. The personal memoirs, which span 40 years, are replete with stories of corporal punishment administered by these Catholic teachers. Dilworth remembers being "rapped on the knuckles for dirty fingernails." Garibaldi believes that corporal punishment, such as the paddling at his school, existed because teachers believed that discipline was "a means to greater end" and that the cruel vestiges of racism and segregation required African American children to be more disciplined and better prepared than their white peers. Garibaldi, in fact, believes that African American parents sent their children to Catholic schools because the teachers had the reputation of being able to enforce a strict code of discipline. However, one of the lessons to be learned from this work is that those of us who were subjected to corporal punishment have never forgotten the humiliating and painful tactics that Catholic teachers used to reinforce their rules. In spite of their commitment to mission and moral convictions, this type of discipline, as Ellis tells us, "kills children's spirit."

Foster suggests that the focus on discipline and order, with the accompanying religious prescriptions, was not necessarily a conflict for African American parents, who believed that adherence to the particular tenets of Catholicism was less important than the school's moral training and character building, with its attention to honesty, integrity, achievement, persistence, and hard work. Dilworth recalls that one of the reasons her mother wanted her children to attend Catholic school was to "put the fear of God into us."

Current research stresses the importance of high teacher expectations for African American students. A prevailing theme throughout these chapters is that Catholic teachers had high expectations for their students. Guided by their sense of mission to teach, save souls, or escape the fires of hell, Catholic teachers were unrelenting in their expectation that all students would and could achieve. Garibaldi summarizes the feelings of most of the authors: "The teachers taught all students as if they could learn, and excuses for unsatisfactory academic performance were unacceptable." The teachers, as remembered by Foster, were "tough, demanding, and insistent." An important piece of this, however, is that the teachers' high expectations were matched by equally high expectations by parents. I recall that my parents were as zealous about and more committed to my achievement than the nuns. Polite, in describing the parents of St. Frances, says that the school represented "the last hope for improved educational opportunities for their children." Foster recalls how her grandmother's recollection of past injustices motivated her family to send her to Catholic schools in order for her "to take advantage of the improved opportunities for Blacks they believed were on the horizon."

The role of parents and family in Catholic schools was critically important. Their role was to support the school in enforcing its religious mandates, supervise homework assignments, get their children to school on time, and raise funds for the school's support. Parents had no role in curriculum decisions, governance, or other matters of management. In current school reform efforts, this type of involvement is either not acknowledged or devalued. However, Siddle Walker's work (1993) on a pre-*Brown* "good segregated school" confirmed that the high degree of parental involvement in this school was attributed to the fact that parents saw their role as attending school functions and responding to the requests of school personnel, not attending to issues of governance and management of the school.

The parents of this book's authors made great financial sacrifices to send their children to Catholic schools. This factor cannot be overlooked as a reason for the success of Catholic schools. When children see their parents' limited time and financial resources being used to send them to private schools, perhaps they respond with increased effort. The question for public school reform is: Are there ways that schools can get parents involved in their children's schools whereby this sense of ownership and investment is re-created?

RACE AND IDENTITY

In all the chapters, the authors struggle with issues of race and racial identity. The stories chronicled in this book span the late 1950s to the early 1990s. The Catholic schools attended by the authors were located in big cities and small towns, and the faculty in these schools were all Black teachers, all white teachers, or integrated faculty. In spite of the variety of place, time, and context, the stories corroborate the finding that African American children learn a lot about race and their racial identity as well as how other children, school personnel, and society define and value racial differences. School personnel must acknowledge the importance of these issues by examining the overt and hidden curriculum as well as their formal and informal interactions with African American students.

The pre-*Brown* stories written by me and Foster tell of teachers who seldom acknowledged children's African American heritage. Foster states that her family sought to instill a strong sense of racial identity in her and it was not assumed that the school should assume this task. I write that the combined efforts of my family, the African American community, and the African Methodist Episcopal Church provided "cultural centeredness" for the development of my racial identity.

During the civil rights movement, Garibaldi's experiences were different. In 1967, the Josephite Fathers actively challenged the vestiges of segregation; however, he left the seminary because he believed he could make a greater contribution to the Black community outside of the priesthood. Dilworth, who was the only Black child in her school from kindergarten to fifth grade, felt as if she was "carrying the load for an entire race of people." Her parents, concerned about her racial identity, decided that she should attend a public high school instead of a Catholic one. During this era, Delpit recalls the Black nuns' "whitewashing" treatment and the nuns' preference for children with European features and light skin as opposed to children who had more African features and darker skin.

The post–civil rights stories of Tate's and Ellis's defiance and direct challenges are in stark contrast to the stories of the other writers. Ellis claims that she was "treated like a slave who needed to be seasoned." Tate openly challenged one teacher and refused to apologize or retract his position. In fact, Tate believes that his Catholic schooling taught and nourished his spirit of civil disobedience through Holy Angels Black liberation theology, which had a strong positive influence on his life, particularly as the theory was embodied by the social activist principal, Father Clement.

Ellis, like Tate, had a similar African-centered orientation but attended a traditional Eurocentric school. Her chapter is essentially a story of the struggle and pain of a race-conscious African American student whose teachers refused to understand the totality of her racial and cultural identity.

This book has presented readers with some lessons for the education of African American students. The lessons are that African American students profit from a demanding curriculum, regardless of the nature of that curriculum or the particular pedagogical approach, that this curriculum must be taught by individuals who are mission-oriented and believe that African Americans must (not simply can) learn and achieve in schools. African American parents and their families must share the values and mission of the school and support the school in ways that are mutually agreed-upon and negotiated. Schools must also acknowledge and identify with their students' African American heritage and understand that African American students are not simply colorful prototypes of white students but students who strongly identify with their culture.

Finally, this book, according to Foster, has also disputed conventional views that assume that African Americans are involuntary minorities who are helpless and hopeless victims in a marginalized culture in constant opposition to dominant mainstream beliefs and practices. The authors, through their personal stories, critiques, historical analyses, and research reviews, have challenged static functionalist theorists, who fail to understand and account for the particularistic ways African Americans respond to imposed societal conditions in order to educate their children. Obviously, the education of African Americans occurs in complex social arrangements in which school, family, and community often operate in both complementary and contradictory relationships. Cremin (1976) has reminded us that "individuals come to educational situations with their own temperaments, histories, and purposes, and different individuals will obviously interact with a given configuration of education in different ways and with different outcomes. Hence, in considering the interactions and the outcomes, it is as necessary to examine individual histories as it is to examine the configurations themselves" (pp. 37–38).

REFERENCES

Baker, S. (1982, December). *Characteristics of effective urban language arts teachers: An ethnographic study of retired educators.* Paper presented at the meeting of the American Reading Forum, Sarasota, FL.

Bryk, A. S., Lee, V. E., & Holland, P. B. (1993). *Catholic schools and the common good.* Cambridge, MA: Harvard University Press.

Cremin, L. (1976). *Public education.* New York: Basic Books.

Irvine, J. J. (1990). *Black students and school failure: Policies, practices, and prescriptions.* Westport, CT: Greenwood.

Jaynes, G. D., & Williams, R. M. (1989). *A common destiny: Blacks in American society.* Washington, DC: National Academy Press.

Jones, F. C. (1981). *A traditional model of educational excellence.* Washington, DC: Howard University Press.

Quality Education for Minorities Project. (1990). *Education that works: An action plan for the education of minorities.* Cambridge, MA: MIT Press.

Siddle Walker, E. V. (1993). Interpersonal caring in the "good" segregated schooling of African American children: Evidence from the case of Caswell County Training School. *Urban Review, 25,* 63–77.

Sowell, T. (1976). Patterns of Black excellence. *The Public Interest, 43,* 26–58.

About the Editors and the Contributors

THE EDITORS

Michèle Foster is Professor in the Center for Educational Studies at the Claremont Graduate School. She is the recipient of numerous awards, fellowships, and honors, including a Spencer Postdoctoral Fellowship, several Spencer Small Grants, a Carolina Minority Postdoctoral Fellowship, and the Early Career Achievement Award of the American Educational Research Association. She has over 30 publications, and her articles have appeared in such journals as *Theory into Practice, Language in Society, Linguistics in Education, Educational Foundations,* and *Educational Theory.* Her edited volumes include *Qualitative Investigations in School and Schooling* and *Unrelated Kin: Race and Gender in Women's Personal Narratives* (co-edited with G. Etter-Lewis). Her own book, *Black Teachers on Teaching,* will be published in 1996.

Jacqueline Jordan Irvine is the Charles Howard Candler Professor of Urban Education at Emory University and the director and founder of CULTURES, the Center on Urban Learning/Teaching and Urban Research in Education and Schools. She has been named the 1992 Distinguished Woman Scholar by Virginia Commonwealth University, the 1992 recipient of the Georgia State University College of Education Distinguished Alumni Award, and the 1992 Outstanding Alumni of Howard University. Her specializations are multicultural education and urban teacher education, particularly the education of African Americans. She has over 50 publications, including her book *Black Students and School Failure* (1990). She has served on the editorial boards of *Journal of Curriculum and Supervision, Journal of Negro Education,* and *American Education Research Journal* and continues to work with public school systems across the country.

THE CONTRIBUTORS

Lisa D. Delpit is the Benjamin E. Mays Professor of Urban Educational Leadership at Georgia State University. Her research has focused on the education of children of color and the pedagogical knowledge of teachers of color. Her published works include *Other People's Children: Power and Pedagogy in Multicultural Classrooms,* as well as articles in leading educational journals. Her work has earned her a "genius" award from the MacArthur Foundation, the 1993 Alumni Award for Outstanding Contribution in Education from the Harvard University Graduate School of Education, and the 1994 AERA Cattell Award.

Mary E. Dilworth is Senior Director for Research for the American Association of Colleges for Teacher Education and also serves as Director of the ERIC Clearinghouse on Teaching and Teacher Education. She is responsible for the development of a number of research and equity projects and publications. She received a B.A. in elementary education and a M.A. in student personnel administration in higher education from Howard University and an Ed.D. in higher education administration from the Catholic University of America. She has written numerous articles and reports, most notably, *Teacher's Totter: A Report on Teacher Certification Issues* and *Reading Between the Lines: Teachers and Their Racial/Ethnic Cultures,* and edited the AACTE/Jossey-Bass publication *Diversity in Teacher Education: New Expectations.*

Kimberly Charrisse Ellis grew up in the Hill District of Pittsburgh, Pennsylvania. After graduating in the class of 1990 from Oakland Catholic High School, she earned her B.A. in African and African American studies and English at Emory University in Atlanta, Georgia in 1994. She is currently working on her master's degree in English at the University of Connecticut and will graduate in May of 1996. In addition, she is seeking her doctorate in American studies and would like to open an independent school for the primary education of African American students. She dedicates this chapter to her mother, Freda Carolyn Ellis, who has been Kimberly's main source of inspiration in getting a formal education, often reminding her daughter that "education is the one thing no one can take away from you once you have it."

V. P. Franklin is Professor of History at Drexel University in Philadelphia. He is the co-editor of *New Perspectives on Black Educational History* (1978) and author of *The Education of Black Philadelphia: The Social and Educational History of a Minority Community, 1900–1950* (1979), *Black Self-Determination: A Cultural History of African-American Resistance* (1992), and numerous essays on African American history and education. His most recent book is *Living Our Stories, Telling Our Truths: Autobiography and the Making of the African-American Intellectual Tradition* (1995).

Antoine M. Garibaldi is Vice President for Academic Affairs and Professor of Education at Xavier University. He is the author of 10 books and monographs, and more than 60 chapters and scholarly articles on

Black colleges and universities, African American males, minority teacher recruitment and retention, and urban education issues. Some of his recent books are *The Education of African-Americans* (co-edited with Charles Willie and Wornie L. Reed, 1991), *Teacher Recruitment and Retention* (1989), *Educating Black Male Youth: A Moral and Civic Imperative* (1988), and *Black Colleges and Universities: Challenges for the Future* (1984). He received his B.A. magna cum laude from Howard University in 1973 and his Ph.D. in educational and social psychology from the University of Minnesota in 1976.

Janice Ellen Jackson is Deputy Superintendent for the Boston Public Schools and former Deputy Assistant Secretary for the Office of Elementary and Secondary Education in the U.S. Department of Education. Her professional career has included two positions with the Archdiocese of Milwaukee—Director of the Office for Black Catholics and elementary school teacher—and positions as an instructor at Marquette University and the University of Wisconsin–Milwaukee. She holds a B.A. in sociology and elementary education from Marquette University, a M.Th. in Black Catholic studies from Xavier University of Louisiana, a M.S. in administrative leadership from the University of Wisconsin-Milwaukee, and a M.S. in administration, planning, and social policy from Harvard University. She is a doctoral candidate in Harvard University's Urban Superintendents Program.

Vernon C. Polite is Associate Professor in the Department of Education of the Catholic University of America (Washington, D.C.). He specializes in research focused on organizational change, school leadership, minority issues, and qualitative research methods. He has held a number of key administrative positions in both public and Catholic schools, serving as a principal at the elementary and secondary levels, federal programs monitor to the U.S. Territory of the Virgin Islands, and director of the Boston public schools' desegregation plan. He has provided professional development workshops for middle school principals affiliated with the Edna McConnell Clark Foundation's Program for Student Achievement. Currently, he provides in-depth technical assistance in the area of institutional reform to Universidad Metropolitana (San Juan, Puerto Rico) and the University of Texas (El Paso) through the National Science Foundation's Model Institutions of Excellence.

Portia H. Shields joined the Howard University School of Education (HUSE) in 1974 and became its seventh Dean in 1993. She holds a Ph.D. in early childhood/elementary education from the University of Maryland, College Park. After serving as Director and Chair of Undergraduate and Graduate Education and Chair of the Department of Curriculum and Instruction, she left HUSE in 1989 to serve as Director of Medical Education and Biomedical Communications in the University's College of Medicine. Among her professional affiliations, she serves on the Steering Committee of the Council of Great City Deans, as a Holmes Group Team Leader, and as a board member of the Association of Colleges and Schools of Education in State Universities and Land Grant Colleges (ACSESULGC) and the Carnegie Foundation's National Project Thirty Alliance. Since April 1995, she has served as Vice Chair of the Goals 2000 Panel in the District of Columbia.

William Tate is Assistant Professor in the Department of Curriculum and Instruction at the University of Wisconsin–Madison. He is also a principal investigator at the National Institute on Science Education sponsored by the National Science Foundation. He is a member of the editorial review boards of the *Journal for Research in Mathematics Education* and *Readings on Equal Education*. He was the recipient of the University of Wisconsin's Anna J. Cooper Postdoctoral Fellowship (1991–1992). His article "Race, Retrenchment, and the Reform of School Mathematics," published in *Phi Delta Kappan*, reflects his thinking on educational equity and mathematics. His articles "School Mathematics and African American Students: Thinking Seriously About Opportunity-to-Learn Standards," published in *Educational Administration Quarterly*, and "Toward a Critical Race Theory of Education" (co-authored with Gloria Ladson-Billings), published in *Teachers College Record*, reflect his interest in the political dimensions of African American education.

Darlene Eleanor York is a partner in the Orion Project, an Atlanta consulting firm. She has taught at Emory University, the University of Georgia, and Agnes Scott College. She is the author of several publications, including her book *Cross-Cultural Training Programs* (1994).

Index